27

27

The Voice of the Yankee Fans

Dr. Joan Fallon

Illustrations James Fiorentino

Written By: Joan M. Fallon
Illustrations: James Fiorentino
Front Cover Illustration: James Fiorentino
Back Cover Photo: Darren Brestin

Library of Congress Control Number: 2005910012
ISBN: Hardcover   1-4257-0228-7
                             Softcover   1-4257-0227-9

To order additional copies of this book, contact:
Xlibris Corporation
1-888-795-4274
www.Xlibris.com
Orders@Xlibris.com
26247

CONTENTS

DEDICATION

To my dad, who gave me baseball and the Yankees, and to my mom, who gave me my athleticism, an appreciation for winning, and a love for the aesthetics and importance of sports. And to James Edward Fallon, the next generation!

ACKNOWLEDGMENTS

No book about baseball or about the Yankees could be complete without a mention of my "baseball buddies."

So to my baseball buddies Ken Nanus; Richie Feltenstein; David Fredston-Hermann; Ann McEvily; Pat McEvily; the Hollanders Alan, Wendy, Michael, and Adam; Joel (for the opening day); Greg Mallozzi; Guy Riekeman; Darren Brestin; Luke and Vincent Belcastro; Eliot Foster; Billy McDevitt; Jennifer Acocella Feltenstein; Josh and Lindsay Tanis; and all the children who come to my office and bring me everything and anything "Yankee" they can find.

And no book about the Yankees would be complete without a mention of my greatest Yankee protagonist and Boston Red Sox fan Kathleen Carten, who had her day in the sun in 2004, but whose search for no. 27 is way out of reach. Thank you for keeping me humble.

And to Donna Cameron and Dan Roble, the only two Red Sox fans who I would possibly take to Yankee Stadium. Thank you for your friendship!

A special thank you is saved for James Fiorentino whose illustrations grace the pages of this book. His talent is as grand as his spirit. His enthusiasm as grand as his heart! He is a special person, and this book project would not have been the same without his phenomenal artistic talent which "screams: GO YANKEES"! I am honored to have met him and to call him a friend.

Thank you James.

PROLOGUE

You got to get twenty-seven outs to win.

—Casey Stengel

Twenty-seven is a significant number to Yankee fans as each game brings us closer to our goal. In researching this book, I came across many references to 27. Some references have significance and should be mentioned before we go on to examine the Yankees' search for their twenty-seventh world championship:

- 27 outs for the perfect game
- 2 + 7 = 9 innings in a game
- Cy Young averaged 27 wins during the course of his career.
- Nolan Ryan pitched for twenty-seven seasons.
- Most consecutive games lost by a pitcher: Anthony Young: 27
- Twenty-seven years after Jackie Robinson entered baseball, Frank Robinson became the first black manager.
- The U.S. Constitution has twenty-seven amendments.
- The two most common symbols on the computer keyboard "@" and "&" are 2 and 7.
- The twenty-seven-star flag became the official United States flag on July 4, 1845.
- Nelson Mandela was jailed for twenty-seven years. A poem by Abena Buscia, a famous poetess, speaks to the twenty-seven years of his imprisonment.
- The element cobalt, which is YANKEE blue in color, has an atomic weight of 27.
- A baby in utero can open its' eyes for the first time in its twenty-seventh week—just in time to watch a Yankee game!

FOREWORD

Being from New York is generally both a blessing and a curse! New York is one of—if not the most—influential, powerful, and bustling cities on earth. Known for its food, its culture, Broadway, the Financial District, Yankee Stadium, the Statue of Liberty, the Metropolitan Museum of Art, The Museum Of Modern Art (MOMA), the Plaza Hotel, and what was once the World Trade Towers, the scene of one of the most heinous crimes on the face of the earth (the terror attacks of September 11, 2001), New York has come to represent the spirit and the embodiment of human strength and perseverance.

While that spirit and that perseverance have come to be the blessing of New York; the curse comes from sharing the city with millions of daily commuters, the fight to drive one's automobile sometimes two to three blocks, and the fast-and-furious pace of daily life with all its stresses. High prices, large taxes, waiting in line, and generally just being one of many make New York its very own unique place. Sinatra in the famous song "New York, New York" belts out, "If I can make it there, I can make it anywhere. It's up to you, New York, New York." That battle cry has become the symbol of all of New York; and indeed, it is played in all its splendor in the Yankee Stadium after every game, albeit differing versions depending upon the outcome of the game.

It is these very qualities that make the New York Yankee fan a unique breed of personage. Much is made of the athlete who comes to play in New York who "can't take the heat" or "the stress of playing in New York." While the media glare in the faces of the athletes is intense and often critical, that heat is fan generated.

As the intensity of the fans and desire for the team to do well spills out all over the city, it places the athlete in a mind-set of winning as an important part of the game. When an athlete comes to New York from what is called a "small market" team, their focus often must change. The thrust of their playing for a small-market team or for a non-contending team may have centered around their own personal achievements, their own place as the "hometown hero." Without the "supporting cast" necessary to put them into the playoffs, personal statistics become important. Put that same athlete in New York, and their focus *must* change. The Yankees are *expected* to win. Winning then becomes the player's focus; and personal achievement, home runs, etc., are not as important as driving in runs or getting on base. The basis for achievement changes.

Never has this type of thinking been more evident than in the case of Alex Rodriguez (A-Rod). A-Rod—who has inarguably been the best player in baseball during the late 1990s and into the early 2000s (twice league MVP, batting champion, a Gold Glove—winning shortstop), as well as the highest-paid baseball player in the land—turns his life around, leaves Texas to join a contender. In doing so, he gives up his Gold Glove—winning position to come to the Yankees. He comes not to be a hero but to be a winner, one of the guys, one of the group of highly skilled players who can bring to New York another world championship. He is expected to be a team player—and an outstanding one.

New Yorkers, while embracing A-Rod with all the kudos that such a fantastic player rightly deserves, want to make sure that while A-Rod is welcomed, his presence didn't *tread* on their "treasure" Derek Jeter. Indeed, not only did the Yankee organization assure Jeter, the "crown jewel" of the Yankee organization, that his position was safe and that he is "the captain," New York fans also stood their ground in feeling the same way. After all, Jeter has four World Series rings, and New Yorkers never forget!

Alex Rodriguez (A-Rod) makes his presence known during the 2005 season.
PHOTO CREDIT/ BRESTIN

So A-Rod came to New York in 2004 and slipped right into third base. He is elected as the starting third baseman at the All-Star game even though he never played the position. He ultimately won a Gold Glove in 2004 at the position that was completely new to him. A-Rod brought with him an element of class and grace to a Yankee team that already was full of classy players.

So the naysayers who thought that A-Rod would take over "Jeter's team" or that the Yankees would seek to "replace" Jeter were wrong. In fact, there appears to be a great camaraderie between the two both on the field and in the dugout. A-Rod was clearly here to win a championship. The 2004 team, it appeared, was destined to win that twenty-seventh championship just after his arrival. After all, A-Rod was here, and the Curse of the Bambino was alive and well! At one point, the team was 9.5 games ahead of Boston late in the season.

The story of the 2004 season will haunt many of the Yankees and Yankee fans for a long time. Those who have championship rings understand the breakdown of energies and lack of focus that ultimately led to the breaking of the Curse of the Bambino and the first Red Sox world championship in eighty-four years.

The 2005 Season was a difficult one for the Yankees. While off to a slow start, they trailed Boston until the next to the last day of the season when they won the American League Eastern Division Championship. They however could not beat the Aneheim Angels in the Division Series. Although A-rod had an MVP season, he could not come up big in the post season. This will ultimately be his test in the future.

This text is written to examine what it takes to win that twenty-seventh world championship. It is about the makeup of a team, about the "collective consciousness" of the Yankee fan, and it is about winning.

The Yankee fan is a unique and special type of person. We will see why Yankee fans are special, why the Yankees are special, and why the Yankees have the most loyal following in all of sports.

CHAPTER 1

THE FRANCHISE

There is no secret that the Yankee franchise is the most valuable one in all of sports. Recognized on seven continents, the Yankee logo has become a symbol of winning. I have traveled the globe, and it never fails that I see a Yankee cap or logo somewhere. From Tasmania to Romania, from Japan to Tibet, I have seen the Yankee logo worn proudly.

And while we will see later that everyone loves a winner, the Yankee tradition of winning is longer and stronger than any other team in the history of sports. Some of the superstars associated with the Yankees' winning through time are some of the most recognizable individuals in U.S. history:

Babe Ruth	Lou Gehrig
Tony Lazzeri	Joe Gordon
Frank Crossetti	Red Rolfe
Tommy Henrich	Bill Dickey
Hal Chase	Frank Baker
Joe Dugan	Red Ruffing
Jack Chesbro	Lefty Gomez
Waite Hoyt	Herb Pennock
Mickey Mantle	Joe DiMaggio
Billy Martin	Yogi Berra
Thurman Munson	Allie Reynolds
Phil Rizzuto	Roger Maris
Joe Page	Elston Howard
Gil McDougald	Clete Boyer
Don Mattingly	Willie Randolph
Graig Nettles	Roy White
Reggie Jackson	Dave Winfield
Whitey Ford	Mel Stottlemyre
Catfish Hunter	Ed Lopat
Ron Guidry	Sparky Lyle
Goose Gossage	Paul O'Neill

Ruth and Gehrig enjoying a moment together.
ILLUSTRATION/FIORENTINO

"The Mick"
ILLUSTRATION/FIORENTINO

This list could go on for pages and would certainly include some of those players from today who continue to thrill us on the field.

To date, the Yankees franchise has won twenty-six world championships, thirty-eight American League Championships, and twelve Division Series. No franchise could be in a winner like the Yankees without a fantastic leader. The Yankees have had some of the most illustrious managers, many storied and many crowned; but most importantly, they were winners:

World Series	Win Manager
1923	Miller Huggins
1927	Miller Huggins
1928	Miller Huggins
1932	Joe McCarthy
1936	Joe McCarthy
1937	Joe McCarthy
1938	Joe McCarthy
1939	Joe McCarthy
1941	Joe McCarthy
1943	Joe McCarthy
1947	Bucky Harris
1949	Casey Stengel
1950	Casey Stengel
1951	Casey Stengel
1952	Casey Stengel
1953	Casey Stengel
1956	Casey Stengel
1958	Casey Stengel
1961	Ralph Houk
1962	Ralph Houk
1977	Billy Martin
1978	Bob Lemon
1996	Joe Torre
1998	Joe Torre
1999	Joe Torre
2000	Joe Torre

The winning ways of the Yankees have been mentioned in so many contexts. Over the years, like any business, the franchise has had good years and bad years: years when the Yankees just plain "stunk" and other years when they could be and were on top of the world again—"world champions."

So the franchise has been stocked with fantastic players throughout the years; astute, clever, and special managers; and loyal, intense, and compassionate fans. The Yankee fan can be characterized as a die-hard, never-give-up, "bleed pinstripes" type of person that goes to the Stadium no matter whether the Yankees win or lose, whether they are a great team or a mediocre one.

CHAPTER 2

FAN PSYCHOLOGY

As sport becomes an increasingly larger part of our culture, the psychology of the sports fan becomes a fascinating and an important subject of study. Much has been written and theorized in recent years about the psychology of the sports fan, and therefore, it is important that we examine those writings and the theories proposed by some of the experts before we examine the psyche of the Yankee fan and their role in winning the twenty-seventh world championship.

Brad Locke, a sports journalist in Mississippi, writes extensively about what he calls the various attributes of fans. He has put together a composite of fans that includes fan behavior, loyalties, and composition. He states that fan composition is a "mixture of primary human emotions" as well as "emotions that emanate from the primary ones." He sees the fan as having all or some of the following emotions and makeup. The left column states the attribute that belongs to Locke's categorization and the right column this author's interpretation or example:

HATRED

The various acts of violence exhibited by the fans as witnessed through the attack on the first-base coach Tom Gamboa of Kansas City Royals during a game in Chicago. A drunken-father-and-son duo ran on the field and just began beating Coach Gamboa.

HEARTACHE

The distinct feeling when the team wins or loses and especially when they lose. The feelings are akin to the loss of a loved one.

CONTEMPT

The feeling that the sports fan has when a player is either selfish or appears selfish. This is true of the Red Sox fans who felt that Nomar Garciaparra, while still playing for the Red Sox, claimed not to be 100 percent but should have been willing to play in a 14-inning game with the Yankees. He was severely criticized for not "sucking one up" for the team. (He was soon traded after that incident.)

COMPASSION

The feeling of sadness upon the loss of a life of a player or a feeling upon hearing of a tragedy that occurs to one of the players even though the fan does not personally know the individual. This was evidenced through the loss of Thurman Munson, the Yankee catcher and captain who died in a plane crash. In another example, this past year, when a tragedy occurred at the Central American home of Mariano Rivera. Mariano left the team to go down the funeral and returned to pitch for the Yankees in the playoffs that evening.

ANIMUS

When a fan gets carried away and allows their "animal instinct" to rule their behavior.

This is often seen during soccer matches in Europe when fans get carried away with emotion and riot.

APPRECIATION

Fans love when their sport heroes do well. There is often an outpouring of appreciation for a job well done. A standing ovation can be given either for a fantastic play or even for a fantastic attempt.

LETHARGY

A lack of support for a losing team. Sort of a "fair-weather fan."

LOYALTY

A fan who sticks by their team through good times and bad. That can be considered a "real fan."

VOYERISM

Many will enjoy a "good car wreck" or some other type of adversity experienced on the field by the sports figure: a collision, unconsciousness, a trip and fall, and hard tackle. When the stretcher comes out, the fans often get excited.

VALUE

True fans appreciate the effort put forth by an individual. When one really tries and even fails, their value is increased in the hearts of the sports fan.

IGNORANCE

Some fans pretend or believe that they know the game well even

> though they do not. So many fans
> do not understand the mechanics
> or the politics of the game.

INTELLIGENCE   Joe Torre

Locke's theory states that most sports fans are a composite of many or all of the above attributes. He states, "Fan behavior is a reminder of how flawed we are, yet how much potential for good exists. Outside the arena, when our true selves are uncovered in unguarded moments, pray that someone beyond ourselves is what others see."

This is a somewhat negative picture of the sports fan and the parts of human nature that we all possess to some degree. If the composite of the sports fan is relegated only to the aspects of human nature that are inherent in all of us, I don't believe those aspects of "humanness" alone would particularly make one a fan. While fans can exhibit things such as contempt, hatred, and animus, the majority of fans, and the majority of time most fans spend being a fan, is not wrapped up in those few attributes.

There are other examinations of fan psychology that I think are more applicable to the Yankee fan. Dan Wann, a well-known sports and fan psychologist at Murray State University, has another well-documented theory about "fandom." He has composed a scale of fan participation based on the idea of "social identity."

Wann developed what is called the sports fan identification scale. Through the use of his scale, he boils fan participation down to eight motives that compels an individual to be a "sports consumer." Different from Locke's theory, Wann interjects social mores as well as economic and moral values on his scale.

Sports Fan Indentification Scale

- Entertainment
- Escape
- Economics
- Eustress
- Aesthetics
- Family
- Group affiliations
- Self-esteem

While not all fans fall into each of his categories, Wann is compelled to make us understand that at the "core" of fan participation is the notion of group affiliation and self-esteem. He goes so far as to say that the great "motivator" for all fans is "self-esteem."

In a speech, Wann stated that those who have a strong or high degree of "team identification" will have their moods, attitudes, and actions dictated by how well the team is doing. He further states that those with "low team identification" will care little with how the team is performing. This high-and-low team identification theory can apply in many ways to many fans, but certainly not to all.

Social identity theory states that people are more likely to behave in ways that basically make them look good to others. He carries this notion right onto the playing field with respect to the fan. He theorizes that association with a winning team "allows one's self-esteem to be elevated." He further goes on to describe that the venues for watching sporting events or talking about sporting events allow the fan to have a "common place at which to increase one's self-esteem and to reach a common ground."

This theory is reminiscent of the fraternity argument or the argument for the necessity for "clubs" where membership brings with it a status or a collective sense of identity that elevates one's own self-esteem. While perhaps important in certain areas of life, I don't think this theory applies directly to the Yankee fan.

Jeff James, another sports psychologist from Florida State University, hypothesizes that "sports provides a source of both group and personal identity, as it satisfies basic needs for belonging." We see this fact played out in the various sports venues where everyone dresses like the players. Player jerseys are an important part of our culture. Baseball, football, and even soccer jerseys are not just a part of modern culture but a part of modern couture.

To complete a chapter on fan psychology, one must also look at the work of Cialdini at Arizona State University. He has coined the terms "BIRGers" and "CORFers." "BIRGers" stands for "basking in reflected glory," and "CORFers" stands for "cutting off reflected failure." Cialdini bases his theory on his findings that the students at ASU were more likely to wear the team jersey on Monday in school after a weekend win and less likely if they lose. He theorizes that the fan's self-esteem is tied to the wins and losses of the team and that their identity is completely tied to the team's success. It is easier to be tied to a winner, he theorizes, than to a loser. This is something akin to the fair-weather fan.

He further theorizes that while many—and indeed most sports fans—adhere to these archetypes of being either, many of the most loyal fans, he states, like those of the Boston Red Sox, do *not* adhere to this. He states that the "Red Sox fans wear their losses like a badge of courage."

While the badge of courage, according to Cialdini, often will signal high self-esteem, I believe that in the case of the Boston fans, the "badge of courage" is sign of self-deprecation.

This self-deprecating type of attitude can be evidenced by the lyrics of a song written by the McDonough Band and played in the many pubs of Boston. The song has an eerily tongue-in-cheek but true ring about the behaviors of the Boston Red Sox fans. While hopefully the fans' relationship will change to some degree now that the team has won their world championship, it may be hard to give up the Red Sox scapegoating that has gone on for over eighty years.

This is akin to the "black sheep of the family," or in psychological terms, the Red Sox have become the identified "sick one" in the Boston family. All ills can be blamed on the one person or, in this case, the one team that is a "loser." Everything can be blamed on the perennial subpar performance of the Red Sox.

The song is called "Blame it on the Red Sox" and basically uses the Sox as an excuse for everything that goes wrong in the life of the Bostonian.

Blame It on the Red Sox
McDonough Band

When the boss won't treat me nice, and
When I've overcooked the rice.
When my feet are killing me,
My back is aching, and there's water on my knee.
I'll just blame it on the Red Sox.
It's so easy. Blame the Red Sox.

For everything that's bad,
They're the reason why my mother left my dad.
When I've got troubles, and I need someone to blame,
I'll just blame it on the Red Sox.
But it's only a game.

When my train is running late,
When my trousers irritate,
When I'm hungover, and there's demons in my head,
When the neighbors' big black dog keeps digging up
my flower bed.
I'll just blame it on the Red Sox.
It's so easy. Blame the Red Sox.

For every little pain,
They're the reason I get caught out in the rain.
From Edgartown to Providence to everywhere in
Maine,
We all love to blame the Red Sox,
But it's only a game.

I've been waiting. It's so frustrating.
I'm tired of always learning the hard way.
When I'm looking kind of rough,
When the job can't suck enough,
When there's something always spoiling my view,
When I swear that woman never did once say "I do,"
I'll just blame it on the Red Sox.
It's so easy. Blame the Red Sox.

For everything that's wrong,
They're the reason that the summer lasts so long.
When every day's another day and life's an endless chain,
I just blame it on the Red Sox,
It's so easy. Blame the Red Sox.
But it's only a game.

www.mcdonoughband.com

There are still other theories about fandom. Revolving around the theme of "commonality," Robert Fisher places the fan in a place of feeling close to the player and that the closeness makes them "a fan." This may well be true of those who have a "loose" identity with the Yankees or other teams. Since many of the Yankees teams had either no superstar or many at the same time, those who are casual fans are more likely to be fans because of some type of kinship with the players.

In the past eight to ten years, the Yankee players have been very much involved in their communities in some cases, raising families and participating in activities with their fans. Those activities can be as simple as going to the Home Depot store where there are often "Yankee sighting" or as mundane as dropping the children at school. This would lend some efficacy to this theory about some Yankee fans, especially those who ordinarily would not be fans. When you take your child to school each morning and standing next to you is one of the Yankees or one of their wives, you are more likely to be involved and become a fan. When you share a common interest or bond—the children, for example—you are therefore more likely to be interested in their lives, and that would include the team.

Yet another theory of fan participation is that of San Diego State University professor Robert Mechikoff. Adapted from Clifford Geertz's work, Mechikoff describes the fan who basically lives and breathes and dies with the team and whose entire social identity as well as emotional and psychological identity is related to their attachment to the team. This type of attachment is often considered "outside of the norm."

Another common theory about the sports fan that has been promoted through time is that an individual is a fan of a particular team because of family tradition. This is especially common in cities where there are more than one of the same type of team; so for example, in Chicago or New York where there is an American League and a National League team, you are either a Yankee fan, or you are a Met fan.

Whether you are a Met or a Yankee fan, or whether you are a Chicago Cubs or White Sox fan, it is theorized that it has everything to do with your history. In many cases, the family "tradition" may be a result of whether, for example, your father or mother came from the Bronx or from Queens or whether they rooted originally for the Brooklyn Dodgers or for the Giants. To that end, there will always be the child that decides to root for the opposite of the "family tradition" and thus, in some cases, infuriating the other family members.

Much has been made of this family-tradition fan mould whereby the entire family is a fan of a particular team. So for example, if you live in the Bronx, it is less likely that you will be a Met fan than if you lived in Queens. While other things may come into play, such as the child's psychology that says, "I'm going to be the opposite of what my dad is or what my parents are," the geographic tie can often be strong.

Most recent work by a graduate student at the University of Miami (Ohio) David Mueller speaks clearly to the "social identity component" of being a fan. He has gone a step further in his work to demonstrate that fandom or social identity within a group is multidemntional. This expounds on previous work which described fandom as a social identity issue which has cognitive, affective, and evaluative aspects. Dr. Mueller in his work which is ongoing (2002-present), includes a "psychometric scale" which measures the mutidemtional aspcts of this social identity theory of fandom to include: public claiming of the identity, purchaseing of apparel, fan aggression, and attendance at sporting events.

All of these theories go a long way to explain the many reasons why 99 percent of individuals are fans. It does not, however, describe in full the Yankee fan. We will see in the following pages that a Yankee fan is a unique breed of being, that there are so many qualities of the Yankee fan that are germane to just the Yankee fan, and that these qualities are in some ways intangible and uncategorizable.

CHAPTER 3

BASEBALL IN NOVEMBER

World Series are jewels; they are diamonds, with each one cut just a little differently. So while all diamonds are not cut the same or have the same clarity, in baseball, one thing is very clear: Reggie Jackson has had the mantle of Mr. October placed upon him because of his clutch play in the World Series. His baseball legacy shines, and forever he will be known as Mr. October, and forever he will be remembered as *the* star of the postseason.

Reggie "Mr. October" Jackson
ILLUSTRATION/FIORENTINO

The tragedies of September 11, 2001, left New York stunned and hurting. In the horrible wake of the devastation that the terror attacks leveled on our city and our country, New York was a city left in pain—sad, angry, and bewildered. New Yorkers rallied around to help each other. Everyone had been touched in some way by the tragedies. Either you knew someone who was missing and presumed dead or was touched by someone who had. Life in New York was just not the same and really hasn't been the same since the terror attacks.

During the days following the attacks, New Yorkers were dealing with an enormous number of issues ranging from an ongoing fear of further attack to finding ways to help those who were working at ground zero. The outpouring of help and selflessness was everywhere. The problems too were everywhere, from lack of utilities to shortage of boots for the ground zero workers. In some cases, the banks and other businesses that had their headquarters or computer systems at the World Trade Center had tremendous difficulty. In the case of the banks, dispensing money or giving their customers balances from their accounts was a problem. The Bank of New York, particularly hard hit, had their main servers in the area of ground zero. The bank responded by giving money based on whatever proof of account you could provide. The bank could not have responded better to its customers!

Blue Cross Blue Shield had their main claim processing facility in the World Trade Center. They moved with rapid speed and with tremendous efficiency to pay the many physicians, hospitals, and individuals who were waiting for claims to be processed. They too were incredibly helpful, communicative, and efficient in asking those who submitted claims within the two weeks prior to the terror attacks to resend the claims; and they processed everything with great professionalism. The economy of the area took a large hit. Blue Cross Blue Shield of New York, because of their diligence, allowed many physicans, hospitals, and other health professionals to keep their doors open.

Some could not even return to their homes due to their proximity to ground zero, and all of New York joined in to provide them shelter. The entire population of the greater New York area mobilized into a ready volunteer force. Chiropractors, who were one of the most needed along with mental health professionals, were dispatched to help the workers at ground zero whose bodies and minds were fatigued and stressed beyond what had been imaginable. Never has an attack of such magnitude occurred in this country. Saint Paul's Chapel was the site of a long-term place for respite and care. Every day the workers of ground zero could seek rest or health care within its walls. My sister-in-law, Kathleen Reilly

Fallon, a foot-and-ankle surgeon, volunteered one day a week at the church where she sewed up cuts on the legs of the workers who were regularly cut sometimes right through their boots by the sharp, mangled steel of the fallen towers. She did that for months after the attacks.

So while the entire nation mourned the loss of life as well as the loss of innocence, it was clear that New Yorkers needed a place to focus away from the tragedy. Mayor Giuliani led the city through the aftermath hour by hour, staying in communication with the city and with the nation in what was really unprecedented candor, substance, and consistency. Never before had an incident such as this been communicated to the people in such an expeditious and open way.

One important thing that happened that Fall that allowed us to look away, but for a moment, from the tragedy that stood in our faces like a reflection in a mirror was the presence of the Yankees in the playoffs.

While the Yankees had been in more playoffs than any other team in history, this time they did so under unique and unprecedented circumstances. They found themselves at the center of an opportunity so unique that only after the season could they possibly see how they helped the city and the fans recover and survive the days and weeks after the terror attacks.

Everyone focused their attention on the Yankees. They played not with their caps but with the caps of the NYPD and NYFD. We too sat in the stands with our NYPD and NYFD caps. They were our heroes. While we were at the games, the New York City Fire and Police departments, as well as hundreds of volunteers, were continuing to wade through the rubble to examine what was left of the World Trade Towers. They searched in vain for survivors; they risked their own lives during those uncertain times for the sake of those who had lost their loved ones.

While the Yankees did not win the World Series that year, their fantastic play allowed us for but a few minutes of the remaining season and the playoffs to put tragedy aside and to join with all the other New Yorkers as we rooted for our hometown team. Together we sang the national anthem. We listened to the Irish tenor Ronan Tynan sing "God Bless America." A triumph of human spirit himself, he lifted us with a chill every time he sang.

We watched the American eagle soar through the Stadium, and we watched through the portico of the old Yankee Stadium facade the men and women with guns who were there to protect us. While we cheered, they readied themselves for any type of further attack. While New Yorkers, on the inside, feared yet another wave of attacks, on the outside, the Yankee fans continued to go to the Stadium and to remain steadfast throughout. We sat in the stands with "our mayor" Giuliani and rooted together with him for "our team." We watched as Paul McCartney and other stars came to support us.

McCartney lent his heart and his presence and his voice to this country, to our city, and to our team. We had one of the most vivid views as a city with respect to the support we had; the world, it seemed, poured its heart out for us.

Then there was our team. Every time we thought it was over, that our wonderful "run" during the playoffs was finally done, "our boys" came back, giving us one more victory—one more day—to cheer!

The Yankees won 4 of their last 6 games with wins coming at the final at bat. Bernie Williams hit a 3-run home run in game 1 of the AL Division Series. He took us where we needed to go yet one more time.

We had as a nation rallied around our flag around the symbols of our nation. We showed our solidarity with others; we hung out flags in record numbers; and even I, out in the front window of my office, which looks out upon a busy street, hung a sign that said God bless America!

GOD BLESS AMERICA

Sign 1 in Author's Window

Of course, God Bless America hung in windows all across the United States. As we reached for answers, as we looked for help through our fear, many people turned to a higher being for help, for guidance, and for mercy as we reeled from the attacks.

Meanwhile, as the Yankees moved deeper into the playoffs, they created miracle after miracle. We defeated the Seattle Mariners 4 games to 1 in the AL Series Championship. My next window in the office then said God Bless the Yankees!

> # GOD BLESS THE YANKEES !

Sign 2 in Author's Window

And still we grieved for the loss of those around us and for the tragedy that had befallen our nation. Every evening, after a day of tears and grief and comfort from those around us, we cheered for our team. We knew they were grieving with us and they too shed many tears, but they also knew their job was to entertain to allow for but a few brief moments for the city to take a minivacation from their grief. Scott Brocius took us again a step further with his walk-off home run, and our boys would go on to entertain yet another day the third picture window in my office bore the sign God Must be a Yankee Fan!

> # GOD *MUST* BE A YANKEE FAN!

Sign 3 in Author's window

The World Series that year was between the Diamondbacks and the Yankees. The Yankees lost the series 4-3 with the Diamondbacks scoring 2 runs in the bottom of the ninth off Mariano "the Sandman" Rivera when a Luis Gonzales bloop-hit fell into center field with the winning run crossing the plate. New York was devastated, but we also knew that the Yankees had given us a gift. When all the odds were against our team, they came through night after night to give us something to smile about, something to cheer for, and something to allow us to take a break from the sadness that was everywhere around us.

We had our moments during the series that reminded New Yorkers that even when down, we could come back. In game 4, down 3-1 in the ninth inning, with the ground shaking beneath our feet as we stood in the stadium stands, it was a wonderful sight to watch Tino Martinez hit a home run that tied the score and sent the game into extra innings. And then with the crowd still screaming and still recovering from the goose bumps of the ninth inning, Derek Jeter hit a walk-off home run in the bottom of the tenth inning, winning the game.

Game 5 found the Yankees down to 2-0 in the bottom of the ninth. Down to their last batters and when hope seemed to wane, the Yankee fans once again turned up the noise, and again the concrete in the stadium began to shake and the feeling of hope and wishing and eternal spirit, which the Yankee fans manage to find in times of complete hopelessness. He was once again our unlikely hero; Scott Brocius hit the home run that won the game, and again we found that as fans, we felt as though we had participated in the win. I have never felt the intensity of power between people as I did that night as we watched and cheered and felt the stadium shaking. The yelling, the clapping, and the intensity of the crowd were almost so strong that one could feel that energy carry the ball out of the park for Scott Broscius, for the Yankees, and for us. What an incredible series, and what an incredible fan connection. It was the very first time that I knew for sure that the fans were certainly a large part of the previous twenty-six Yankee World championships.

When one examines the statistics from the series, one could never predict that the scores would be so close. The Yankees managed to stay in the series despite the distractions, despite the pall that hung over the city, despite their performance that was less than stellar from a statistical point of view.

	Yankees	Diamondbacks
Batting Ave.	.184	.264
Hits	42	65
Runs	14	37
RBI	14	36
Pitching ERA	4.41	1.94

And one will ask then, how could the Yankees who were outpitched and outhit during the entire series still be in contention? Well, the answer, I do believe, lies in the hands of the Yankee captain Derek Jeter. Dubbed Mr. November because of his tremendous heroics during the World Series, which extended into the month of November for the first time due to the delays produced by the terror attacks, Derek Jeter is probably one of, if not the greatest, Yankees that ever lived. While so many of his wonderful characteristics will be examined later in this text, it is important to note that he rose above what would be considered normal and customary for a fantastically talented player and gave us spectacular offensive and defensive plays, which will be etched into our minds forever.

Jeter at Bat
PHOTO/FALLON

Mayor Giuliani summed it up best on what the series meant to New York:

> "For us, it was a lot better to have been in the seventh game of a World Series than not to have been in one. It was terrific for the morale of the city, terrific for the spirit of the city, and terrific for the economy of the city. They did everything they could for us, and we are very proud of them."

CHAPTER 4

THE FORMULA

General managers stay up at night trying to imagine the right formula to bring a championship to the hometown fans. If only there was a formula, if only enough money could buy a team, if only the farm system was stocked with more talent, if only I had the skills to make better trades—these thoughts pervade the minds of GMs all winter and all summer, all spring, and all fall. While little is left to the imagination among the elite GMs, the formula for a great team continues to be an elusive concept.

Theo Epstein of the Boston Red Sox doesn't sleep at night thinking about the Yankees. Even with the Sox's 2004 triumph over "the evil empire," I'm sure Theo has been staying up, trying to look at matchups and hoping that his recent acquisitions are sufficient to allow for change and salary considerations, which can be used later. He worries if he has enough to get him to October—enough to beat the Yankees. I'm sure Brain Cashman experiences some of the same things. He and Theo are among the youngest, brightest, and most successful GMs in baseball.

Some GMs have begun to use statistics to guide their acquisitions and to place players on their rosters. Some, like Billy Beane, have very successfully employed this tact. Using hitting as his major focus and signing older talents, mainly college players, to stock his rosters, Billy Beane has brought significant success to his franchise. His successes have been chronicled in the book *Moneyball* written by Michael Lewis.

So what *really* constitutes a *winner*? Why have the Yankees been so successful at winning? When you ask those questions to baseball fans across the country, they will tell you that the Yankees "buy" their teams. They will say that principal owner George Steinbrenner buys his teams, and he doesn't care how much they cost. Of course, while the Yankees do indeed have the highest payroll in MLB, they have not always had that level of payroll, and still they have been winners. Further, presently, the Yankees have the highest payroll in baseball; and it certainly doesn't appear that way hovering around the .500 mark and looking some nights as though they are a Little League team making mental mistakes and errors that do not reflect the status and talent of today's Yankee team.

So I propose here a formula that makes the Yankees a team apart from the others, a team that is destined to win the twenty-seventh and beyond. The components of that formula are the following:

> Player talent
> Management
> Manager
> Team chemistry
> Passion
> Tradition
> Collective charisma
> + Fans
> _____
> WINNER

CHAPTER 5

TALENT

Talent, as we will see, is only one component of the equation. Having talent gives a team options, and those options can be carried into the game as components for winning. I propose here to put talent into an equation that can give a GM a sense of the magnitude of their talent as a function of winning.

A team's potential to win because of player talent and the augmentation of player talent by the presence of other talented players on a team can be expressed as a mathematical function, which is $n!$ or n factorial.

Factorial refers to the number of permutations (combinations) possible for a given or fixed set of numbers. It is therefore the arrangement of objects in a particular order. So therefore the number, strength and position all have import with respect to for example the talent on a baseball team or even a team's batting order.

Assuming an American League team has nine position players and one designated hitter (DH), the team's potential ways of winning offensively are:

$$10! = 10 \times 9 \times 8 \times 7 \times 6 \times 5 \times 4 \times 3 \times 2 \times 1$$

$$= 3,628,800 \text{ ways to win}$$

In exploring this concept further, there is a large difference between having five excellent hitters and having two excellent hitters on a team. Having the larger number of good hitters does not permit the opposing team to "pitch around" the hitters as they might do to the team that has two good hitters. So if the position of the opposite teams was to *walk* all good hitters, then the team with the five good hitters would walk in a run each time the five batters came to bat consecutively. So while this is, of course, a hypothetical situation, having five good hitters does allow the manager to either bunch them together or to spread them apart, depending upon the opposing team's pitching, game planning, or coaching. The manager with the five good hitters therefore has more ways to win than the manager who only has the two good hitters. The same, of course, is true of pitching and fielding.

Further, a team, for example, that has speed can do things like steal bases or hit and run in certain circumstances where teams without the speed cannot. So talent is an important building block for all teams.

So let's look again at talent as an equation. If winning were solely a function of talent, then the team with the best talent equation would win. Winning, as we will discover, has other pieces, other important components, which we will examine later in this text. For our purposes, we will rate the talent of the non-pitchers from 1 to 5, with 5 representing the greatest talent; and we will rate the pitchers from 1 to 5 as well, with 5 as being the best.

We will this time assume a National League team in any one game. In one game, there are eight position players, one pitcher, and one relief pitcher. The maximum strength of talent, assuming all were 5s, would then be

$$11(5)! = 1,949,062,500,000,000$$

A team with talents that are all 3s would exhibit a strength of talent of the following magnitude:

$$11(3)! = 7,071,141,369,600$$

So the difference in the strength of magnitude of the talent component between a team with all 5s and a team with all 3s is 1,941,991,358,630,400.

The difference, of course, is enormous. No team at the major league level is made up of all 3s or 5s. The teams are generally a mixture of all those numbered talents, and not all players will play up to their potential on every night.

So we see that the magnitude of the talent used in the winning equation can change with a simple loss of a player or players where they are replaced with players of lesser talent. So an injury that places a player on the disabled list, for example, will alter this equation. Talent, however, as we will see, is only one component of the winning equation.

While examining talent, we must also discuss further Billy Beane's way of picking talent for his team. While we said earlier in the chapter that Beane looks for hitters who are older who have excellent on-base averages. He does this in the face of the more tried and true "five-tool talent" measures that the scouts are accustomed to using. This traditional system of rating players, long used to evaluate baseball talent and to place that talent into positions on the field is for the first time beginning to break down. In a short summary, players under the more traditional talent rating system are evaluated for their ability to (1) throw, (2) hit for average, (3) hit for power, (4) run, and (5) field.

Each of these "tools" are rated on a scale of 2-8, with 5 being average. Those evaluations render an absolute score when added and also, depending upon which of those talents are the strongest, would determine where they would play on the field.

The first two highest-rated tools that they possess are known as the carrying tools. Each position requires two excellent "carrying tools"; and except for the shortstop position, which requires three "carrying tools," it is those first two "carrying tools" that determine where a player is likely to be strongest—at what position.

For example, whereas a first baseman is required to have his carrying tools be hitting and power, the second baseman needs his carrying tools to be hitting and fielding. The right and left fielders need to have hitting and power, but the center fielder needs to have running and fielding as his carrying tools.

Scouts generally look for five-tool talents and for those who "look like ballplayers" and who fit their preconceived notion of what a catcher or shortstop should look like. In their five-tool system, hitting is the number one carrying tool for five of the eight position players.

If one juxtaposes the two systems against one another and you interchange on-base percentage, as Billy Beane does for hitting average, then many players who would generally be overlooked by other clubs would be picked up by Beane and integrated into his system of winning. So with respect to hitting, in Beane's system, a player who hits for an average of .260 but has an on-base percentage of .450 would rate high in Beane's eyes whereas other teams might pass up such a player.

However one picks talent, it is only one factor in the equation of success for a baseball team. We will continue to examine the others.

CHAPTER 6

MANAGEMENT

When management sends a message to the team and to the fans that is consistent and clear, it helps the team to operate in the healthiest way possible. That, of course, is true no matter what type of business, no matter what the nature of the management is. Like a child who needs encouragement, boundaries, and clear communication, a team needs rules and regulations and messages that are consistent.

Some of the most contentious Yankee teams were the ones that were managed by Billy Martin. Regularly fired and rehired by George Steinbrenner, Billy had one of the most complex and difficult relationships in all of sports between the management and manager or coach. Immediately following Billy, a stream of other managers came and went, all taking some sort of personal criticism doled out to the press by the principal owner.

Billy was hired and subsequently fired five times by the Yankee management. His stints as manager became known as Billy 1, 2, 3, etc. Martin took the Yankees to the World Series in 1976 and 1977, winning the series in 1977.

Subsequent to that turbulent time, the Yankees continued to have a slide when they stocked their teams, which were not winning once, with high-priced free agents. Without leadership either from the management or from the bench, the Yankees were known during those times as the "Bronx Zoo".

The Yankee management then began to send clearer and clearer messages to its teams. Under the general "managership" of Gene "the Stick" Michael and, subsequently, of Brian Cashman, the management of the Yankees has sent clear, consistent messages. Those messages to the players are unmistakable: respect for the players as well as loyalty to the players both past and present. Under the present management, the Yankees have won four World Series and have brought many important Yankees of old back to the Bronx, including Yogi Berra.

27

1st base coach Roy White
with A-rod
PHOTO/ BRESTIN

3rd base coach Luis Soho with
Jeter. PHOTO/ BRESTIN

Further, as consistent with their loyalty message, many of the former
Yankees have come back to be coaches, scouts, and aides. Willie
Randolph, Donny "Baseball" Mattingly, Roy White, Luis Sojo, Joe
Gherardi, Bucky Dent, Reggie Jackson, and others continue to serve in
the Yankee organization. Further, Mr. Steinbrenner has reached out to

players, many of whom have given to New York a great deal of fine baseball but who have not played for the Yankees. He did this with players such as David Cone, Darryl Strawberry, Al Leiter and Doc Gooden. He further finds places for his former players within the organization. He treats the former players like family.

Tino Martinez, a fan favorite was brought back to NY in 2005

For all the criticism leveled at Steinbrenner, he continues to show compassion for aging stars, for those who need a second chance, for those who he believes in, and for those who he feels are part of the Yankee family.

Suzyn Waldman, who is now the first woman in baseball doing in the booth play-by-play/commentary for the Yankee network, YES, tells a story of great compassion and great courage on the part of the Yankee organization. I recall her recounting the story of the summer she was undergoing chemotherapy for breast cancer. She either had to stay back in New York for treatment or receive treatment while on the road as she traveled with the team. George and the Yankees arranged for her to have treatment in every city that they visited, and she was able to continue to do her job. She was unable to work only on the day of and the day after she received her chemotherapy, which she brought with her on the road. She was therefore able to keep up with her chemotherapy schedule while still keeping her Yankee schedule. There are few people who could actually make that happen for Susan, and Steinbrenner is one of those people.

That type of care and concern, as well as her ability to continue working at something she loves, no doubt contributed to her healing. She remains cancer free and is an inspiration to every little girl who is told she cannot do what she wants to do. She was treated as part of the Yankee family and continues to be treated as part of the family, and it is in those messages that the Yankees make a statement.

CHAPTER 7

THE MANAGER

There are many styles of managing. Some styles seem to work in certain circumstances, for certain players, and for certain teams. The wise manager understands his players and finds the easiest way to bring out the best in each. Miller Huggins, Joe McCarthy, and Casey Stengel have had the longest tenures as Yankee managers. Their legendary tenures now sit alongside that of Joe Torre's.

In the first seventeen years of the Steinbrenner era, the Yankees had seventeen managers and a total of nineteen managers in the first twenty-three years. Joe Torre, the present Yankee manager, has had the longest run of any Yankee manager under Steinbrenner and one of the longest of any Yankee managers beginning in 1996 and running through today. Torre has proved to be probably one, if not the greatest, Yankee manager of all time. He has four World Series rings since 1996 and is poised to bring home his fifth and the Yankees' twenty-seventh world championship.

Known for his calm nature and enduring belief in the champion of human spirit, "Mr. Torre," as he is still called by Derek Jeter, commands from his players excellence, honesty in play, and cooperation on and off the field. Although often non-demonstrative especially during the game, he is passionate and deeply cares about his work and his players. He is not afraid to hug a player, and at the same time, he is not afraid to tell them like it is while always encouraging and always evoking the fight and the excellence within them. He consults his trusted advisors and is more deliberate in style, more sure of himself than almost any manager in the major leagues because he listens and understands his players, their abilities, their strengths, and their foibles.

Manager Joe Torre
ILLUSTRATION/ FIORENTINO

He is further able to balance the pressure of the New York press, the front office including George Steinbrenner, and the grind of the day-to-day play and travel of the game. He is a testament and an honor to the game!

While his on-the-field demeanor is a fine thing and his accomplishments are now legendary, he also is not afraid to tackle what is important in life: what takes place off the field. Having formed the *Safe at Home Foundation* with his wife, Ali, Joe Torre confronts the past in a positive and creative way, which paves the future for so many youngsters who are victims of violence at home. While understanding that home should be a safe place, the Torres make a statement that stands to protect all children.

From the Safe at Home Foundation Web Site

There can be nothing more devastating to a child than abuse and violence at home. Home should be a sanctuary, a safe harbor from any storm. Yet, for many children, home is a place of danger and fear of an abusive adult.

Joe Torre knows that fear. He lived it as a child. Even in his formative years, Joe stayed away from home, fearful of his own father, who abused his mother. As Joe became a father himself, he realized that no child should have to live with that fear.

It is in that spirit, and in memory of his mother, Margaret, that the Joe Torre Safe At Home Foundation has been established. The Foundation's guiding principle is that every child has the right to be safe at home.

When one grows up with that fear, they often develop what is known as hypervigilance. This is true not just of children of domestic violence but also of children of alcoholics and children exposed to other dangers. Hypervigilance is defined in the following ways:

- Enhanced state of sensory sensitivity
- Extreme sensitivity to cues that may signal presence of feared object or situation
- Excessive awareness of his/her surroundings so as to "catch" the harm that is approaching

Hypervigilance, which comes from having grown up in a household where he and his siblings were not safe, affords Joe an eye and feel for people, which is unparalleled. While some could live their life in fear and rage after having grown up in those level of circumstances, Joe takes his eye for sensing cues in behavior and the "awareness" of his surroundings and turns it into a sense of his team, and his watchful eye on the opposing team into a winning managerial career.

While I have not personally met Joe Torre, I can bet that his ability to sense the present state of a person or to judge their character by observing their outward movements is phenomenal. So turning that into a baseball eye allows Joe to sense when a player is fatigued long before the player might sense it. It further allows him to gauge the emotional need of a player who may need a start or an encouraging word or just a nod of approval. A word of encouragement at the right time or a pinch runner or hitter at just the critical moment can be the difference between a win and a loss.

Joe *always* seems to make the right moves. Those moves come no doubt from experience, intellect, baseball sense, and some luck. For Joe, you add the extreme sense of being able to read people and use of his hypervigilance, and you have a fantastic manager.

Just the mere fact that he could turn such negative energy in his life into positive energy for himself, his family, and those around him is a wonderful thing.

Joe Torre teaches us that children should not live in fear. He sends a message first to those children who live in these environments of violence and abuse and bullying that they deserve better. He also sends a message to the children that they are not alone, and there is help.

Children who grow up in an atmosphere of anger, violence, and bullying lose their self-esteem easily. Many never get it back; many never grow up to accomplish the things that Joe Torre has. He is a role model for all children. He and Ali should be commended for their efforts in behalf of the children everywhere.

One cannot talk about managers without talking about the coaches who are in so many ways near and dear to the manager and the team. Through the Torre era, he had some of his most trusted aides and great baseball minds at his side. Don Zimmer, his bench coach, brought with him a wealth of experience and baseball wisdom. Mel Stottlemyre, pitching coach par excellence, sits next to Torre in the dugout and helps him to manage the team. The Yankee tradition of excellence and achievement has produced innumerable heroes of the baseball world, and Mr. Steinbrenner has had a penchant for bringing them back to the team in roles ranging from special scout to manager. Spring training has generally brought out the old-timers who get a chance to work with the young talent. For example, the Yankees brought in Graig Nettles to help with A-Rod's transition to third last year during spring training. Nettles's predictions about A-Rod's ability to make the transition were exactly right.

Today the Yankees have Louis Sojo, Roy White, and Don Mattingly in addition to Mel; and now for the first time, he brings into the dugout another valuable Yankee catcher who may be destined to be the heir apparent to Joe Torre, and that is Joe Gerardi. A leader in so many ways, Joe was a valuable addition to the team this year. While he no doubt will get a chance to manage his own team in the very near future, I know he will be back in the Bronx one day soon to manage the team he loves, The Yankees.

CHAPTER 8

TEAM CHEMISTRY

Regardless of how much talent an individual possesses, no matter how much talent a team has, without the proper chemistry, there will be no winning ways. The team's chemistry is one of the issues that are intangible, that are immeasurable, and are completely unique to each set of individuals on a team.

Teams in general will have varied personalities, work habits, likes and dislikes as well as family, health, and other issues, all of which may or may not affect the player and ultimately the team. The chemistry of the team is important as it relates to the various issues:

- timing on the field
- knowledge of what other players are doing
- knowledge of what other players are thinking
- anticipation
- stress of action or inaction
- confidence in teammates' abilities

Billy Beane, who is the general manager for the Oakland A's, has had tremendous success, as we said earlier in this text, bucking the traditional system of scouting and of choosing players. While we examined his basic theory and operation and how he picks talent, we did not address how that talent translates into team chemistry. By choosing players who are older and more mature, that are generally college graduates, he bridges the gap between the older and the younger players. By choosing this type of player, he builds in a level of cohesion, which one might not generally find on a team filled with nineteen- and twenty-year-olds as well as thirty-five- and thirty-seven-year-olds. Immediately, the lack of age as an issue creates cohesiveness. The conversation, the music, the shared common bonds, and the interests will potentially help with team chemistry.

So while team chemistry can come in many forms, it is not unusual to find it in opposites as well. Nowhere can "team chemistry" embodied by a group of seemingly "incompatible," "unusual" guys be looked upon as greater than would be the Boston Red Sox 2003-2004, who won the World Series. Ranging from Pedro "Who's Your Daddy?" Martinez to the ever-dependable, long-haired center fielder Johnny Damon, the Red Sox were a team that embodied the ultimate in come from behind victories, beating the New York Yankees for the AL pennant coming from behind 3 games to 0. This seemingly uncohesive group of "personalities" was able to come together with a chemistry of their own making it to win the AL pennant and the World Series—a feat not accomplished by the Red Sox in eighty-four years.

The Yankee teams of 1996, 1998, 2000, etc., had tremendous chemistry. That chemistry could be attributed to the fact that much of the team rose up through the Yankee farm system and the fact that there were no "superstars" but just players. These wining teams were so special in that the winning hit or play could come from any Yankee in the lineup and Yankee in the field. Whether that be Tino Martinez or Jorge Posada or Scott Brocius, that winning *hit* could come from everywhere. Opposing teams tried to guess often who to walk and who to pitch to but were often unsuccessful because everyone on those teams could deliver.

**Yankees Celebrate another victory.
PHOTO/FALLON**

The chemistry between the team members allowed for positive thinking no matter who was at bat, and it also allowed for the other aspects of the game to be in "sync." Those magical teams and the World Series they won will be a study in all aspects of winning but especially in team chemistry.

CHAPTER 9

TRADITION

Perhaps there is no franchise, no team, no institution, save for the British monarchy, that has more tradition associated with it than the New York Yankees. The winners of twenty-six World Series and the winningest team in history, the Yankees, their stadium, and their story are steeped in tradition. From their uniforms, which bear only their numbers and not their names (unlike other teams), to the way Roger Clemens would touch Babe's monument before every Yankee Stadium start, tradition is synonymous with the Yankee name.

During the playoffs in 2003, the AL Series was tied 3-3, and Aaron Boone who had horrific playoffs prior to that moment of infamy came to bat. Earlier in the evening, it was reported during batting practice and possibly just prior to that at-bat that Jeter told a nervous Aaron Boone that sooner or later, the "ghosts" would show up. The ghosts? Was he talking about Casper, the friendly ghost? No, he was talking about the tradition—the tradition of winning that was embodied by the players of the past. It is now legendary the home run that Aaron Boone hit in the 2003 ALS championship game.

In extra innings of game 7, with the game tied and Boone going up to the plate, Jeter reminded him that the ghosts were out there. Willie Randolph, the third-base coach, reminded Boone as well that earlier in the beginning of the playoffs that he had said that Boone was going to be the hero. But he was such an unlikely hero because his batting average during the playoffs was so terrible that to even conjure up a picture of Boone hitting a monstrous home run seemed preposterous.

Once again, the best thing could have happened to Boone, did. His eye, his strength, and his timing allowed him to hit one of the largest home runs of his life and probably of his career. Some careers are defined by one act; in some cases, like Buckner, it is a negative act, but in the case of Boone, it is a positive one. Whether it was the ghosts or Randolph's continued belief in Boone or not, Aaron Boone did the impossible.

Tradition is everywhere with the Yankees. Thurman Munson, the Yankee captain and star of the 1970s, was killed twenty-six years ago in a plane crash. A man who loved his family and who traveled extensively back and forth between New York and his home just to be with his children continues to be a part of the Yankees each and every day. His locker remains as a shrine to him since his death; and the beloved captain who is gone and who helped them to be champions is still an inspiration, is still a person of storied legacy and stature—a Yankee forever. Further to that, during the 2004 season, Thurman's son proposed marriage to his girlfriend in front of his father's monument in center field. The Yankee tradition carries on.

No talk about Yankee tradition can leave out the Yankee captains. Derek Jeter, who is the current Yankee captain, a designation given to only a few of the greatest Yankees of all time, believes strongly in tradition, respect, and timing. Some of his most incredible "feats," including the diving catches and the "flip," were done at a time where the tide of the game or of the series could change because of his one heroic move. Because Jeter understands the level of tradition that comes with being a Yankee, he is able to transmit that to the others he plays with as well as to the fans.

Yankee Captains

- Hal Chase   1912
- Roger Peckinpaugh   1914-1921
- Babe Ruth   May 20-25, 1922
- Everett Scott   1922-1925
- Lou Gehrig   1935-1941
- Thurman Munson   1976-1979
- Graig Nettles   1982-1984
- Willie Randolph   1986-1989
- Ron Guidry   1986-1989
- Don Mattingly   1991-1995
- Derek Jeter   2003-present

Jeter is another in the long line of players who embodies Yankee tradition. He is followed closely by Bernie Williams, Jorge Posada, and Mariano Rivera, each—all—*Yankee*. Mariano, who signed a new contract last year, did so with little fanfare and with an eye toward being a Yankee his whole life and retiring a Yankee. And those who have been Yankees honor it in a very special way. Old-timers' Day is one of awe and of nostalgia; it is of the young, old and the old old, and even the ancient. It is a thrill for the players and for the fans alike. The Yankees get to renew their friendships, and the fans feel like they are going back to their childhood.

Bernie Williams
ILLUSTRATION/ FIORENTINO

Jorge Posada
ILLUSTRATION/ FIORENTINO

Derek Jeter
ILLUSTRATION/ FIORENTINO

Mariano Rivera
ILLUSTRATION/ FIORENTINO

The following is attributed to Mickey Mantle's speaking about Lou Gehrig as they prepared to retire Mantle's no. 7 on June 8, 1969:

"I never knew how someone who was dying could say he was the luckiest man in the world. But now I understand" (Mickey Mantle).

Both Lou Gehrig and Mickey Mantle lived their last years with grave infirmities, Gehrig with ALS and Mickey with liver disease. These two fabulous players were an inspiration during their playing days and also during their last days, as they devoted their efforts to public awareness of their infirmities.

As I spent my childhood reading biographies, my favorite was always Lou Gehrig's. I can remember as a very young child a vivid memory of my parents letting me stay up really late one Friday night because there was no school the next day to watch the Lou Gehrig story.

Lou Gehrig
ILLUSTRATION/ FIORENTINO

Mickey Mantle was my hero. He was the hero of so many who grew up in the fifties and sixties. His tremendous physical prowess and his humble nature made him a favorite of so many. Of course, he was also well-known for his drinking and the liver disease he ultimately succumbed to, but for those of us who watched him play, he was the Mick—he was "our Mickey."

Mickey Mantle
ILLUSTRATION/ FIORENTINO

As an adult and a doctor, I felt great compassion for Mickey as he awaited a liver transplant. Not given to writing letters to celebrities, I wanted him to know that watching the Yankees helped me through my childhood and that his struggles even on the field during those last years when he moved from the outfield to first base did not go unnoticed, especially by me. That letter was written almost two years before his death. Some months after his death, I received a call one day from the Mickey Mantle Foundation, telling me that they were going to publish a book of letters written to Mickey and that he had picked mine out for the book prior to his death. You can imagine how significant an event in the life of a fan that moment was for me to know that somehow I had touched the life of Mickey Mantle as he had touched mine. The book, *Letters to Mickey,* has since gone out of print, but every Yankee fan should own a copy. They are still available.

Mickey had many attributes that are rarely discussed but I think are germane to this text and that are important to the legacy and the future of a team that has won as many championships as the Yankees have.

There are a few quotes that I think sum up the "specialness" of the Mick. This is one quote of his own:

"Out of all of my achievements, awards, and honors, all I want to be remembered for is as a great teammate" (Mickey Mantle).

The other is by Johnny Blanchard, a teammate who States:

"He was friends with everyone on the ball club. If you had a bad day, Mickey would wait for you in the clubhouse, and he'd tap you on the shoulder and invite you out to dinner. The next day, you'd go out and get four hits" (Johnny Blanchard).

And then, of course, because of his extreme love for the Yankees, for the game, and for the tradition, Mantle has said:

"Playing eighteen years in the Yankee Stadium is the best thing that could ever happen to a ballplayer" (Mickey Mantle).

Lou Gehrig, another Yankee of tradition, who was one of the greatest Yankees to ever grace the Stadium, found himself in the midst of an illness from which he would never recover; and as he reflected back on his life, he used the infamous words that would ring forever in the hearts of all Yankee fans.

Below is the speech he gave on that famous day:

Fans, for the past two weeks, you have been reading about the bad break I got. *Yet today I consider myself the luckiest man on the face of this earth.* I have been in ballparks for seventeen years and have never received anything but kindness and encouragement from you fans.

Look at these grand men. Which of you wouldn't consider it the highlight of his career just to associate with them for even one day? Sure, I'm lucky. Who wouldn't consider it an honor to have known Jacob Ruppert? Also, the builder of baseball's greatest empire Ed Barrow? To have spent six years with that wonderful little fellow Miller Huggins? Then to have spent the next nine years with that outstanding leader, that smart student of psychology, the best manager in baseball today, Joe McCarthy? Sure, I'm lucky.

When the New York Giants, a team you would give your right arm to beat and vice versa, sends you a gift, that's something. When everybody down to the groundskeepers and those boys in white coats remember you with trophies, that's something. When you have a wonderful mother-in-law who takes sides with you in squabbles with her own daughter, that's something. When you have a father and a mother who work all their lives so you can have an education and build your body, it's a blessing. When you have a wife who has been a tower of strength and shown more courage than you dreamed existed, that's the finest I know.

So I close in saying that I may have had a tough break, but I have an awful lot to live for. (Lou Gehrig)

Today, the deadly disease that Lou Gehrig suffered from bears his name. Amyotrophic lateral sclerosis (ALS) is most often referred to as Lou Gehrig's disease. It has appeared in some ways to be selective for athletes. A cure is sometime away, but Lou Gehrig epitomized with strength and dignity how someone with a degenerative disease should live and die.

So we see that the Yankee tradition in triumph and in tragedy is alive and living in the hearts of the Yankees through time. That same level of tradition lives in the hearts of the fans as well. The Yankee tradition is strong and a very significant element of the life one lives as a Yankee fan. We will examine the fan element in the next sections.

CHAPTER 10

COLLECTIVE CHARISMA

For the purposes of our equation for success, talent, chemistry, and tradition of a team can often translate into what I call collective charisma. Collective charisma is aggregate of character and ability in a team that far exceeds what one individual could exhibit alone.

In the last four Yankee world championships, the level of "collective charisma" was so high that it almost defined the team. The only other team in the most recent times that exhibits similar charisma is the New England Patriots, who just won the last 3 out of 4 Super Bowls. Led by their young "replacement" quarterback Tom Brady, who has become almost a legend, and their other players like Ty Law and Teddie Bruski, who, unlike other teams, often play both offense and defense, exude that level of collective charisma. Wonderful players on the field and community and civic-minded in their off-field activities, their collective charisma is experienced by all New Englanders.

One of the most outstanding moments in sports that I have witnessed took place at the opening day on 2004 at Fenway Park. As part of the opening ceremonies, the Red Sox stood around home plate in a semicircle; and the Patriots, dressed in street clothes and many with their jerseys on, walked in from center field with the Vince Lombardi Trophy in hand. They literally went to each Sox player and touched them with the trophy, almost as if they were anointing them or trying to get their "good luck" and fortune to rub off on the Red Sox. So whether that ritual worked or not, the level of collective charisma that came from the Patriots was evident just by the way they walked onto the baseball playing field at Fenway that day.

It is said of the Yankees that many managers in the major leagues will impress upon their young players to watch the Yankees as they play, as they warm up, and as they go about the business of playing the game: confident, self-assured, but without that "cockiness" or "swagger" that is possessed by so many athletes. The most successful teams of these modern

Yankees have been fielded by those who grew up Yankees: Jeter, Bernie, Mariano, Posada. All Yankees from the start, all farmhands, and likely to remain lifetime Yankees.

Collective charisma is a part of the team makeup that is often very appealing to the fans. Beyond a winning record, this type of "charisma" will draw the fan to a team because of the desire to emulate, the desire to be liked, the desire to dream about being just that "cool." Many of the Yankees teams through the years have had collective charisma. It is a term that can define both the Yankees of today and the Yankees of "yore."

Living within commuting distance to the stadium and being a part of the fabric of the local area, "Yankee sightings" are common. What is most uncommon is that the fans' interactions with the players off the field are very positive ones, with the players responding to the fans in generous, patient, and fun ways. There are so many examples of where the Yankees, as individuals, have touched the lives of people that I know and have endeared themselves to their fans.

Last season, I went to watch one of my little patients play a Little League game. His team happened to be playing the team who had Mariano Rivera's son as a player. What was striking to me was the way in which Mariano conducted himself at the game. He intently watched the game. Once the game was finished, he went up and shook hands with every player on both teams and with every parent who also wanted to shake his hand. He stayed behind to sign every last autograph that was asked of him. He signed the bats, balls, etc., for the kids with patience, with grace, and with dignity.

Similarly, a few years ago, one of my patients was at Columbia Presbyterian Hospital for a stem cell transplant for multiple myeloma. Her teenage daughter was visiting her, and as she entered the lobby, she saw Derek Jeter there. He was there as part of the work of his Turn 2 Foundation. She went up to him and shook his hand, and he asked her why she was visiting the hospital. She went on to describe her mom's condition.

Derek immediately recounted to her the fact that Mel Stottlemyre, the Yankee pitching coach, received a stem cell transplant for the same problem as her mom's, and Mel was doing very well. He then turned to her and said, "Hang on a moment." He went over to the information desk and asked for a piece of paper. He then asked her what her mom's name was, and he wrote her a note that said,

Dear Pat,
>   Please get well soon.
>   Derek Jeter

My patient found the note to be a treasure as she spent many weeks getting prepared for the transplant and then many weeks recovering. She is still doing well to this day, and her grandson has Derek's autograph as his treasure.

One of my best friends is a real estate appraiser. He goes to do a walk-through of a house with a prospective buyer. The buyer turned out to be Joe Torre. Joe too was most gracious and was all too happy to go to his car and get a picture and autograph it for his son. I have had more than one of the patients come into my office and tell me that they were on line to get a coffee or a bagel or an Italian hero in the deli up the street with Joe Torre in line with them. He always made time to acknowledge the fans and to give them an autograph if they asked or even stop to chat for a few minutes.

Bernie Williams is another one of the "core" Yankees. A Yankee from the beginning, Bernie will go down as one of the greatest Yankees of all time. Right now, he sits close to the top five in almost every category of Yankee achievement. He is one of the most underrated players to ever wear the pinstripes, and his clutch play and his great big heart will be as much admired as his four rings and his stats. The following are just some of Bernie Williams's outstanding achievements as a Yankee as compared to other outstanding Yankees:

Games played:	Mantle
	Gehrig
	Berra
	Ruth
	Williams

Hits:	Gehrig
	Ruth
	Mantle
	Williams

At bats:	Mantle
	Gehrig
	Berra
	Williams

RBIs:	Gehrig
	Ruth
	DiMaggio
	Mantle
	Berra
	Dickey
	Williams

Doubles:	Gehrig
	Mattingly
	Ruth
	Williams

Runs:	Ruth
	Gehrig
	Mantle
	DiMaggio
	Williams

Home runs:	Ruth
	Mantle
	Gehrig
	DiMaggio
	Berra
	Williams

Total Bases:	Ruth
	Gehrig
	DiMaggio
	Mantle
	Berra
	Williams

Base on Balls: **Ruth**
                     Mantle
                     Gehrig
                     Williams

**Bernie Williams
PHOTO/FALLON**

The list goes on, and he may move up in many of these categories before his playing days are over. "Bernie Goes Boom" with the Bee Gees' "Disco Inferno (Burning, Burning)" playing in the background will hopefully happen many, many more times

As good a ballplayer as he is, he is as nice a person, as fine a teammate, and as great a human being as one will find. He is only too happy to sign whatever someone leaves for him in the local deli when he stops to get his coffee or tea in the morning. My sister-in-law, who lives in the same small town, left him two balls to sign: one for me and one for her baby son. Neither was an official major league baseball. Bernie left word that the balls would be more prized if they were official major league baseballs and that she should go out and buy those and he would be happy to sign those for her.

John Flaherty who opens his home and backyard to children in the neighborhood, or Scott Brocius who always made sure that all the kids in the neighborhood where he lived were able to see at least one Yankee game during the season, have not gone unnoticed. Scott so often gave tickets to children who he didn't know but whom the locals told him might not be able to afford to attend a game during the season.

These types of community interactions and spontaneous giving from the team make for a type of collective charisma. That collective charisma is only enhanced by the "clean cut" and team-spirited actions that the Yankee organization promotes. In addition to the clean-cut, no-facial-hair, short-haircut look that the Yankee organization demands, it further does not allow contractual "perks," such as private jets, special rooms on the road, etc., which other teams routinely give their "superstars." The lack of differentiation and the cohesiveness of the team make for a special form of "collective energy." That energy translated into a type of charisma is felt on and off the field and pervades the players, the stadium, and the crowd.

Children often find themselves "in trouble" when they try to be "cool," when they try to emulate adult behavior, or when they look to their friends who they feel are cool. Looking at the Yankees' collective charisma can give a child a role model and something positive to emulate.

"Collective charisma" is about a group of individuals whose sum is greater than its parts, whose whole is complete, unassuming, aware and yet not enamored with itself.

CHAPTER 11

PASSION

Passion is a very important part of the game of baseball. Without passion on the part of both the fans and the players, the season becomes much too long and the effort much too great. From the perspective of the players, the daily grind of playing, the travel, the separation from the families during the time when the children are off from school, and the continual maintenance of their playing rituals make it difficult to be an outstanding player without passion for the game.

The word "passion" is often used in various ways, but "passion" defined is: the purposeful emotional engagement or commitment to work. From the Latin for "bearing" it has in the past been associated with "suffering". Passion further defined as being reflected in an increased willingness to go over and above what the job normally calls for.

With passion for one's work, it can do many things:

- makes work fun
- keeps you motivated
- inspires others
- makes you productive
- makes you successful

One cannot teach passion, and one cannot learn passion. Often thought of as the "fire in one's belly," it keeps the player working at their craft day in and out. Without passion, the player is relegated to rely on their talent and the circumstances of their play. Without passion, little is created by the player beyond what is their talent. With passion, the results of their energies and the fruits of their talents are much greater.

The word is often used as conjunction with a crime that is said to be committed out of passion. Generally, that reflects on someone who commits a crime out of impulse and without self-control or reflection, and without thinking of the consequences. In a baseball sense, when a team is said to be "tight"—where they are not playing to their full potential, making errors, not hitting, etc.—it may be that they have lost their passion. Passion allows the player to play reflexively and to use as much of their talent as possible. Passionate players do not play tight.

When you have passion, you are playing "in the game", immersed in the moment. When you play without passion, you play outside the game. Thinking too much and trying too hard are not elements of passion and only serve to create errors and a lack of hitting. As with a pitcher, a pitcher with passion will pitch; without passion, the pitcher is just throwing the ball.

This passion is also true of the fans. Without the emotional engagement and commitment to the team, the fan is incomplete. What sets the Yankee fan aside from other fans is their passion for the team. To paraphrase something A-Rod said when he first came to New York, when asked about the difference between New York fans and other fans he has found in the cities where he has played, he said in the other cities, the fans might be sad that the team lost; in New York, he said the fans don't sleep if they lose.

This passion of the Yankee fan can be seen in the enormous level of discourse that takes place between the fans about "their team", in the level of attendance at "the stadium" as well as in the great amount of clothing and other Yankees items purchased and worn during the season as well as all year long.

The Yankee player such a Jeter who dives for the ball who runs into the stands who goes that extra mile for his team is clearly full of passion. That passion sets him aside as a GREAT player!

CHAPTER 12

THE YANKEE FAN

The last part of the equation for success and the building of the twenty-seventh, twenty-eighth championships, and beyond is the Yankee fan. The Yankees, more than any other team, have a unique and phenomenal fan that is unparalleled in sports. In the previous chapter we looked briefly at the passion of the Yankee players and the fans, that passion is only one component of the fans. While the Europeans are avid soccer fans and they become involved in rooting for their teams to such an extent that the fervor can carry them into violence in the stands. The Yankee fans' fervor is somewhat unique. Some of those qualities are the following:

- male and female
- not age specific
- not year or team specific
- nonviolent
- respectful
- obsessed year round
- go to the ballpark
- in love with their team
- wear team uniforms year round
- often wear jerseys of retired players, living and dead
- "bleed pinstripes"

While these attributes may seem common, they are not. The *level of specificity* of engagement of the Yankee fan is what makes them unique. The intense love affair is carried on during summer, fall, winter, and spring, whether the team is a wining or losing one. If the team is in the postseason or winning in special ways, more fans will often notice, but the regular fans will always be there. So somewhere in the back of all New Yorkers' minds is the thought of the Yankees.

During the winter, the mere mention of a number, say 38 or 75 or 101, between fans has a very specific meaning. So for example, if I were to receive an e-mail and the body of that e-mail said one thing— 76—I would certainly know that it meant 76 days until the opening of spring training and the reporting of pitchers and catchers. The winters are long for the Yankee fans and even longer when they are not in the World Series or when they lose the WS. This year, the Yankees placed a counter on their Web site so that the fans could just turn to the Web site to see how many days until pitchers and catchers report to spring training. The ritual of New Yorkers flocking to spring training is a long-held one, and even bigger is the opening-day ritual where Yankee fans from near and far flock to the Bronx to see their "Bronx Bombers" open their season.

Opening day is generally what I call a "testosterone filled" ritual where every young man within one hundred miles of Yankee Stadium will skip work or school to go to "opening day." Absenteeism is at an all-time high in the tri-state area (New York, Connecticut, and New Jersey) for this bonding ritual. For the Yankee fan, the hope always is that the opening day will not fall on one of the two big religious holidays that could potentially come around the time of opening day: Easter or Passover. While Passover presents a special problem for the hot dog eater, Yankee Stadium does accommodate those of the Jewish faith by serving kosher hot dogs during the season. During Passover, the Jews do not eat leavened bread, which precludes the eating of the hot dog buns.

Once opening day has occurred, the Yankee fan then has six solid months of baseball. Multiple trips to the Stadium, Bat Day, Cap Day, Old-timers' Day are just some of the milestones that mark the Yankee season.

The Yankee fan has been likened to the tenth man on the field, the tenth batter in the lineup, the secret weapon of the franchise. Intensely loyal and intensely vocal in the ballpark, the Yankee fan has more than once "carried the ball out of the park."

A New Yankee
fan Jennifer
in her wheelchair
PHOTO/SUZANNE
FELTENSTEIN

The playoffs and the World Series at Yankee Stadium are special times. The electricity and the energy are so large, so powerful that having been there to witness that the energy of the event in front of me, unfolding as a storybook open with pages turned, the Yankee Fan can and has pushed the ball out of the stadium, has allowed the bat to "get around" faster, and will—I suspect—continue to help the team win games.

One only needs to be at the stadium during the playoffs to feel the energy, the shaking of the concrete in the stadium as the fans are clapping and stamping their feet to see how that energy pushes the Yankees. Mariano, on the mound in the ninth inning, 3 outs away from the end of the game, and the crowd, already worked up from the playing of "Sandman", starts to shout and yell and clap in such way that the cutter cuts farther, that Mariano throws it ninety-three miles per hour instead of ninety-one miles per hour, that the batter he faces becomes more and more anxious as he feels the crowd cheering. Timing, strength, and will can be altered by the collective energies of the Yankee fans. If you talk to a Yankee fan who has been there during those times, each will tell you this story: that the energy that is generated from the fans is so high and so powerful that it defies definition.

On any given day at the stadium, many of the fans will be decked out in team clothing, shirts, and jerseys, with the numbers or names of their favorite player emblazoned on the back. The thing that is most noticeable is that the loyalty to the players present and past is huge. So it would not be unlike a typical game at the Stadium to find many fans with Tino Martinez's name and/or number on their shirt. Tino has four rings with the Yankees, and until just this year, he was traded away for Jason Giambi. His loyal fans never forgot his contributions; and of course, he is back among us, quietly going to finish his career most likely a Yankee.

Tino Jersey
PHOTO/ FALLON

Ruth, Gehrig, Mattingly, Righetti, Torre, Munson, Jeter, Matsui, Mickey, Maris, and all the old and present players will be represented in uniform at the stadium.

Player Jersey Collage
PHOTO/ FALLON

The love for the players and the fans' loyalties to those players is huge. For example, one of the best and most talented Yankees to *never* wear a ring is Don Mattingly. Multiple-time batting champ and Gold Glove winner, Don Mattingly retired with a "bad back" one year before the Yankee run of four world championships. It was indeed Tino Martinez who was brought to take his place. The Yankees embraced Tino while at the same time remaining loyal to Mattingly. Dubbed as "Donny Baseball," that name says more about the player Don Mattingly than almost anything. Donny Baseball, of course, is presently the Yankee hitting coach and will hopefully be around for the twenty-seventh, twenty-eighth, and more world championships. When announced as a coach, especially that first time, Mattingly was cheered louder than almost everyone except for

Derek Jeter. Mattingly gave the team something to cheer for during the lean years, during the years when the Yankees were not the winningest team in baseball. Don Mattingly embodies the collective charisma—he was an intensely loyal and a fierce competitor—and the Yankee fans *never* forget his contributions to their lives.

The loyalty, the intensity, and the joy of the Yankee fan will help this team to win yet another championship. The tradition of the Yankees will live on in the children as they too become Yankee fans. With so many young girls now involved in sports since Title IX came into effect, the advent of YES, the cable TV station of the Yankees, and the presence of Suzyn Waldman in the booth will attract a whole new breed of loyal Yankee fans. I'm sure the Yankees can look forward to generations of fans both male and female.

Knowing the intensity of my fandom, when my nephew was born, my sister-in-law looked at me in the delivery room and said, "I don't know anything about my son except one thing: *that he will be a Yankee fan!*"

The beneficiaries of the collective charisma are the fans. The loyalty of the fans, which is undying toward the Yankees, is fueled by the collective charisma because it allows for identification and even, in some cases, "transference."

The *Merriam-Webster* dictionary defines "transference" as "the redirection of feelings and desires and especially of those unconsciously retained from childhood toward a new object."Because this is actually a distortion of reality, it often has a negative connotation. And also because many of these retained feelings and desires are negative, their expression can often be looked at as negative. In psychoanalysis, as the patient expresses these feelings toward the therapist, it begins to cast the therapist into a specific role such as that of a parent or spouse. The patient begins that transference when they feel bonded enough to the therapist to do so. As the patient begins to project those feelings and they then can begin to learn to control those feelings or work through them, the psychoanalytic process is deemed working.

To this end, as transference signals a bonding between two individuals, there is a level of transference that occurs between the Yankees and their fans. The bonding that takes place comes from the identification of the fans with both the players and with their collective charisma. They not only see themselves as little boy or girl baseball players, but they also see the "good guy" nature of the players and find an intense identification. As that identification becomes a bond, it then becomes transferential.

Much can be said about the transference between the Yankee players and their fans. This bonding and transference, as we will see, plays an important role in bringing no. 27 to the Bronx. The "coolness" of the Yankees, the examples they set, and the level of identification with the fans are all important aspects of the "winning formula."

CHAPTER 13

YANKEE FANS FOR THE AGES

No book centered on the Yankee fans would be complete without a mention of certain fans that epitomize the loyalty and tenacity of the Yankee fans.

Bleacher Creatures

Many of the teams in the major leagues have active and special bleacher fans, but the Yankee bleacher fans have their very own unique flair and composition. They are most famous for throwing and encouraging the throwing back onto the field of any home run hit by an opposing player. They will yell for the "lucky" fan to throw it back until they do, or the fan will face many minutes of heckling and booing from fans across the stadium initiated by the bleacher fans.

At the beginning of every game, the bleacher "creatures" make their mark by calling out the name of each Yankee player on the field until the player acknowledges them with a tip of the hat or a wave of the glove. Once the player acknowledges them, a large cheer goes up from the bleacher crowd.

The chants sound like this:

Der—ik Jeeee—ter. Der—ik Jeeee—ter
(for Derek Jeter)

or

Teeen NO   Teeen NO
(for Tino Martinez)

or

Mat—sue—eee   Mat—sue—eee
(for Hideki Matsui)

The Bleachers

One of the most interesting things is that the entire rest of the stadium allows only the bleacher fans to perform the ritual. After attending a home game where this is the ritual, one leaves wondering, "Is this a ritual because of the extreme outreach of the Yankees or because no fan is too small or pays too small an amount for a ticket to be ignored by the players?" In either case, the bleacher creatures have made their mark, and a Yankee Stadium game would not be the same without them.

Freddy

Freddy is an icon at the stadium. With his hat and his frying pan turned drum, he walks the stadium in the late innings, banging away for his Yankees. You can often find him early in the evening outside the stadium, banging away on his "drum," and late in the game, walking through the stadium after having been given a ticket by a departing fan.

If you listen carefully during any one game, you can hear the clang of his spoon against his frying pan. Always adorned with colorful homemade signs, Freddie will be clanging away throughout the stadium. And oh, if you want to, Freddie will allow anyone, especially small children, to have a clang or two on his drum. Just ask.

Sustained by donations and the occasional free ticket from a season ticket holder, Freddie even has a newsletter that you can subscribe to, but I think it is only for "donors."

Freddy and the author
PHOTO/BRESTIN

One of the most faithful and staunchest of fans is former mayor Rudy Giuliani. Sitting in his box just to the side of dugout behind home plate, the mayor and his family are frequent visitors to Yankee Stadium. While the New York Knicks have Spike Lee as their fan icon, the Yankees certainly have America's mayor Rudolph Giuliani. And I can guarantee you that if Reggie Miller played baseball, Rudy would be in his face just like Spike Lee! Thank you, Mayor Giuliani; thank you, Spike Lee; and thank you, Reggie Miller. We will miss you and so will Spike!

The Grounds Crew

Well, one might ask why I would look at the grounds crew as a "special fan." It is not so much the fact that the crew members are fans—which I'm sure they all are—but the fact that their deep and enduring interaction with the fans makes them a fan icon.

Grounds Crew YMCA
PHOTO/FALLON

Firstly, the Yankee grounds crew is and has been one of the finest, if not the finest, in baseball. Exceedingly efficient in the days when a measure of salt of the grounds crew was how fast they could roll and unroll the tarp for the infield during rain delays, the Yankee crew still holds the mark. In an age when so many of the stadiums are covered or have retractable roofs, Yankee Stadium, for being located in the northeast, is extremely well-cared for and is playable when other fields would certainly not be.

That being said, one of the highlights of the Yankee game comes in the fifth inning when the grounds crew comes out to rake the infield and do so to the tune of "YMCA." Known as the "Dragsters," this crew comes out and sings and "dances" to the tune of the Village People's "YMCA," performing all the moves along with sometimes fifty-five-thousand-plus cheering fans. It is one of those moments when generations come together as mothers and sons, daughters and fathers—all—are singing "YMCA," performing the requisite alphabet moves.

CHAPTER 14

THE SIGHTS, THE SOUNDS, AND THE SMELLS

One of the most important parts of the "Yankee experience" are the sights, the sounds, and the smells of the stadium and the surrounding area. Located in the South Bronx, the New York City Borough of the Bronx just north of Manhattan, the Bronx has experienced a significant demographic change over the past fifty years. The migration of the Jews from the Grand Concourse and the Italians from Arthur Avenue and the Irish from Bedford Park has left that part of the Bronx in a socioeconomic crisis. Fordham Road, once a bustling shopping area, experienced a loss of business in the mid to late seventies; and immediately, the migration north into Westchester had begun and continues until today. This left the area around the Stadium run-down with multiple vacant buildings and a high unemployment rate. Street crime and drug sales were common, and attendance at the Stadium began to decline.

In the mid-eighties, the area around Yankee Stadium began slowly to change. The location of the courthouse nearby continued to call the legal profession from all over New York State to come to the South Bronx on a daily basis. George Steinbrenner took over the majority ownership of the team, and the winning Yankees of Reggie Jackson and Thurman Munson began to overtake the area, and fans began to return. One only has to walk the blocks around Yankee Stadium during the playoffs to recognize that it is one of the most electric places on earth. From the street vendors hacking their wares to the stores along River Avenue selling Yankee everything—from jerseys to hats—you can feel the excitement before you enter the stadium.

The bars along 161st Street and River Avenue are overfilled with fans, trying to cool off on a hot summer day or trying to get warm on a cold October night before a playoff game. If you listen, you can hear the wails of Gerard Szigethy yelling for patrons. His deep baritone voice permeates River Avenue as he announces the fact that the restaurant that he works for has cold water, cold beer, and hot dogs. Why pay stadium prices when you can get the beer for half the price? he says.

Stan's is doing a brisk business, selling Yankee merchandise of every sort. If you need the latest jersey or warm-up fleece, Stan's has it. If you need an authentic hat of the proper size, it is Stan's where you want to be. So many of the other stores along those two avenues carry everything you could possibly want. Just walk around and look.

So you are walking from the Court Deli where you and your "Yankee buddy" just had dinner with two unrelated other "Yankee buddies." You eat the biggest corned beef and tongue sandwich, or Reuben, in the Bronx or two kosher hot dogs and baked beans and coleslaw; and you stop at TWINS next door because your teenage son is in there, eating four or five hot dogs because he couldn't stand waiting in line at the Court Deli. You proceed down the hill to River Avenue where you can hear Gerard Szigethy, a fixture calling patrons into the restaurant, and the crowd is getting larger and larger by the minute as the subway dumps hundreds of fans right at the foot of the stadium.

You now wind your way past thousands of fans all going in different directions as you make your way to the entrance gates and through the metal detectors (during the playoffs) and on to your seats.

You look out onto the field, and you spy the most beautiful playing field in all of baseball Yankee Stadium. Every Yankee fan can tell you about the first time they entered the Stadium and what it felt like to see that beautiful green grass, the white facade, and the crack of the bat during practice. Just looking out onto the field can give one the goose bumps.

A walk out to the monument park gives you the goose bumps all over again because you can remember the days that the monuments were in play, something our children will never know, and you think back and remember the day that Mel Stottlemyer hit an "in the park" home run behind those monuments. Oh, maybe you can't remember whom he hit it against, but you sure do know who was pitching for the Yankees.

And then you hear Bob Shepherd, and you again get the goose bumps because you hear that voice and you know what he is going to say:

Welcome to Yankee Stadium!

And then you know the beginning is coming, whether that be the national anthem or the rush of the Yankees onto the field led by their captain Derek Jeter; you know that there is baseball in the air and that 27 is sure to follow!

Yankee Stadium
PHOTO/FALLON

THE FUTURE

In 2005, which was Joe Torre's tenth season as manager, the Yankees had a total home attendance of over 4 million. And while the Yankess clinched the AL East Division, on the second to last day of the season, they were eliminated in 5 games in the division series by the Aneheim Angels. It was a disappointing season in many respects and an exciting one as well.

As the season did not result in an appearance in the World Series, it did see the emergence of the next wave of young Yankee farmhands who may just be destined to be the next Bernie, Mariano, Jeter, and Posada.

The Yankee tradition will continue on through the generations; and the fierce loyalty and the participation in the postseason and the cheering, I suspect, will not stop anytime soon. The Yankees are poised to win yet another championship in the near future. Perhaps it will be 27 in 2006. The Yankee fans will soon start cheering!

The Yankee Lineage
PHOTO/ R. BRESTIN

PHOTO/ ILLUSTRATION CREDITS

Front cover	Original Watercolor James Fiorentino 2005	
1	A-rod Photo	Darren Brestin
2	Ruth and Gehrig Illustration	Fiorentino
3	The Mick Photo	Fiorentino
4	Reggie Jackson Illustration	Fiorentino
5	Window Sign	Fallon
6	Window Sign	Fallon
7	Window Sign	Fallon
8	Derek Jeter Photo	Ken Nanas
9	Arod and White Photo	Fallon
10	Jeter and Soho Photo	D. Brestin
11	Tino Martinez Photo	Fallon
12	Joe Torre Illustration	Fiorentino
13	YankeesWin Photo	Fallon
14	Bernie Williams Illustration	Fiorentino
15	Jorge Posada Illustration	Fiorentino

16	Derek Jeter Illustration	Fiorentino
17	Mariano Rivera Illustration	Fiorentino
18	Lou Gehrig Illustration	Fiorentino
19	Mickey Mantle Illustration	Fiorentino
20	Bernie Williams Photo	Fallon
21	Jennifer in her wheelchair	S. Feltenstein
22	Tino Martinez Collage	Fallon
23	Team Jersey Collage	Fallon
24	Bleacher Photo	Fallon
25	"Freddy and Author" Photo	D. Brestin
26	Yankee Grounds Crew	Fallon
27	Yankee sign Photo	Fallon
28	"Brestin Boys" Photo	Randi Brestin

POSTSCRIPT

Things happen very quickly in New York. Well into the 2006 season, the New York Yankees are truly in a great position to win their 27th World Championship. "The Boss" has already predicted a World Series win, and the players continue to be upbeat and excited, despite some plaguing injuries. The pitching, while perhaps not considered by the pundits to be "stellar", is by my estimation thick, enthusiastic and seasoned. When combined with their fabulous offence, one which should produce more runs per game than any offence in the history of baseball, the season again looks promising. The season is; however, long, and the road is "rocky" (excuse the cliché'), but the path to their 27th World Championship is laid out and clearly within reach.

The Yankees have made some off season moves which again prove that they are a class organization, one which demonstrates a loyalty to their players, as well as a keen instinct in the pursuit of the finest in baseball. They clearly understand what it takes beyond monetary considerations, what it takes to procure the keys to the winning formula. The signing of Johnny Damon and Bernie Williams is just another one of those really cool things that the Yankees always manage to accomplish. With pre-season tendonitis already having reared its head for Damon during the World Baseball Classsic, the retention of Bernie is even more important to the Yankees than it appeared in the off-season. Bernie had a great World Baseball Classic playing DH for Puerto Rico, and hopefully he will remain in great shape and healthy as the season progresses. Watching him playing right field, then left, should be an example of a team player one who understands what it takes to win!

With the official coming of the Season, we look forward to our "boys" once again coming into our living rooms nightly. While 27 is a distinct possibility, anything can happen in the game of baseball. We are just glad the season is here!

HEREEEEEEEEEEEEEEEES . . . . JOHNNY!

What do Babe Ruth, Waite Hoyt, Wade Boggs, Red Ruffing, Carl Mays, Sparky Lyle, Danny MacFayden, Everett Scott and Johnny Damon have in common? . . .

Each was traded directly to the Yankees from the Red Sox, and each (and Damon remains to be seen) went on to have an illustrious career with the New York Yankees.

Signing with the Yankees in the off season as a free agent, Damon now gives the Yankees and the Yankee fans exactly what they had wished for: the signing of the future (at least the immediate future) in Johnny Damon; a proven leadoff hitter and "gamer", while still retaining the services of our beloved Bernie Williams for at least one more year. This unprecedented move allows Bernie to retire gracefully as a Yankee either this year or maybe even after next year or two, and allows the team to have an everyday centerfielder, who is also a fine leadoff hitter. Not since the departure of Chuck Knoblauch, the leadoff hitter during the most recent string of Yankee World Series victories, have the Yankees been able to win it all. Damon puts Jeter down one slot in the batting order and allows him a breather and gives more versatility and breath to an already power lineup. It allows Jeter to hit for more power and play hit and run with Damon in a way he couldn't do as the leadoff hitter when he was more concerned with just getting on base.

The powerful line-up could look something like this:

Damon	C
Jeter	SS
A-rod	3B
Sheffield	RF
Giambi	1B
Matsui	LF
Williams	DH
Posada	C
Cano	2B

Any set of three batters can produce runs, and every opposing pitcher must constantly realize that they do not get a break in this lineup.

The signing of Bernie and Johnny, who both have the same agent, Scott Boras, is from my perspective, one of the coolest moves in all of baseball. How could one of the toughest agents in the game, Scott Boras, represent two different players both of whom in essence would be vying for the same position on the same team? I kept asking myself and others "isn't it a conflict of interest, how could he represent both players if they are vying to play the same position on the same team"?

While no one I could find, even some astute attorneys, had given the scenario any thought, and couldn't answer my question, I finally decided (to myself) that the only way Boras could play his hand was to go for a 2 for 1 deal, where the Yankees signed both players each for their respective contributions to the team. Damon would then be the everyday player and hit leadoff, and Bernie, who is in the twilight of his career to DH, would play center and the outfield on occasion. While I do not know for sure this is true, in my mind it became a win-win situation where the players win, the agent wins, the team wins, but most of all the fans win! The Yankee fans get to have their beloved 5 time all-star and 4 time gold glove winner for at least one more season, AND Damon too!! Wow, that worked for me!!

Damon played 5 years in Kansas City, one year in Oakland and 4 years with the RedSox. Interestingly enough, his last year with the Royals and his last year with the Red Sox were his best years with respect to batting and field averages. In Kansas City his batting average the first year was .282, and ended up in his 5th and final year at .327 with a slugging percentage of .495. During his stay with the Sox, his first year hitting average was .286 and in his final year with the Sox, which was last year, his average was .316. So Damon clearly starts off slowly and revs up over time.

I personally think it will take him a very short period of time to become accustomed to his new surroundings and predict that he will be as good this year as he has been in the last 2 years in Boston. If he stays healthy and his shoulder tendonitis does not keep him out of play, it should be a very fine year for Damon and the Yankees.

Johnny Damon was an icon in Boston. With his long hair flowing outside of his cap, he dove, rolled, leapt and played center field with the heart of a champion. Hopefully his next championship will be in pinstripes.

"DR." DONNIE BASEBALL

While we are on the subject of the future of the Yankees, nothing appears to be more important than the presence of Don Mattingly in the dugout. While mentioned earlier in the text, it appears that Mattingly is going to make enormous contributions to the team while at the same time learning all that he can from a manager that has everything to teach.

Mattingly has never managed in the major leagues, he has never managed in the minor leagues, he has never managed in any league. He has not been a GM, and he has been out of the game since his retirement, until 3 years ago when he agreed to be the hitting coach of the Yankees. A humble yet astute student of the game, Mattingly has those qualities that will always make him a leader, that will make him always one of the most admired Yankees to ever wear the uniform.

So while he will forever be a fan favorite, his numbers were cut short and resulted in an abbreviated career due to a bad back that plagued him all through his career. A lefty thrower and lefty batter, Donnie had one of the purest lefty swings to ever hit the ball over the porch in right field at Yankee Stadium. His glory years were the years that I was growing up, and every youngster who ever put on a glove during those years wanted to be Mattingly. I think that soon a whole new generation of youngsters are also going to want to be Mattingly as you see him study the game from his fantastic mentor Joe Torre, and hopefully Mattingly too can help coach his Yankees to another World Championship.

One of the most remarkable changes that I have ever seen in any sport is the change in Jason Giambi during the 2005 season. Embroiled in the steroid controversy, and "outed" by some, Giambi turned his life and his game around and much of that credit has to do with Don Mattingly. Mattingly turned a dead pull power hitter, and made him a hitter with tremendous power. His entire swing was changed to such a degree that he doesn't even look like the same man at the plate.

Instead of swinging up at the ball, in a sort of "upper cut". Or "swipe-type" fashion: that typical "lefty swing". Giambi learned from Mattingly to swing across his body. Not only did his strikeout numbers go down, but he began spraying the ball all over the field, and hitting for power at the same time. No longer is that extreme overshift to the right side of the infield as effective. His new swing, coupled with his great eye for pitches, makes Giambi a whole new player.

Giambi who played basically only part time in 2005, ended the season with 32 home runs and 87 RBI's. His average climbed all season, and he was named the American League's comeback player of the year in 2005. He earned the respect of his peers, of his manager and coaches. Once the trade winds swirled around Jason, and now he is one of the most beloved Yankees. The fans respect him for what he has done.

"Donnie Baseball" who worked tirelessly with Jason during the 2005 season still waits for his first championship ring. We know he has 10 empty fingers and hopefully the 2006 Yankees can give him his first ring this October.

After having spent much time with Bubba Crosby, a reserve outfielder during Spring Training 2006, Bubba showed great potential until his most recent injury. Bubba's ability to hit has been so dramatically enhanced, and when coupled with Mattingly's complete Giambi "makeover", Mattingly has been termed "Dr. Mattingly" by Suzyn Waldman; a name quite apropos.

I think we are going to see "Dr. Mattingly's" handiwork all season, and every Yankee fan will certain enjoy the results!

MESSAGES FROM THE READERS . . . .

One of the most touching parts of writing a book like this one, is the responses that I have received back from the readers. Here is an example of one response I received which appears to sum up the many responses I received:

"Wow! What a statement! What a Legacy! The book is Fantastic!
It connects with the inner/true Yankee aspect of being a Yankee fan. I know how wordy I can get but that aspect of connecting with something greater than yourself . . . is a transcendence. What do we want to do with our patients? A better connection with their inner self, a stronger connection with their creator? Well my dear fanatic . . . that what you have done for us . . . please note that not everyone who picks up this little ditty will receive a full portion of Yankeeosity, but those who recognize the beautiful illustrations, those who feel the ride of mentioned victory, and those who feel the hollowness of losing, will treasure this book . . . on behalf of my children, and all the younger Yankee fans, thank you for creating something that we can share, relate to, and most of all; hand down to others . . . as Ralphy used to say to Alice. . . .
Baby . . . you're the greatest!!

EF

BOB SHEPHERD, EDDIE LAYTON, ROBERT MERRILL, KATE SMITH, COTTON EYE JOE(EY) ET.AL.

In the basic portion of the text I wrote about the sights the sound and other parts of the "Yankee Experience". While I felt as though I had captured most of the salient elements of the Yankee world, others who read the first edition mentioned to me that I had "missed" some of their favorite elements, some of the parts that make The Stadium experience something special for them. So I felt it was important to mention them here as part of the postscript.

Bob Shepard has been the voice of the Yankees now for 56 years. Part of THE YANKEE EXPERIENCE as I grew up was Bob Shepherd as the voice, Robert Merrill singing the anthem, and Eddie Layton at the organ. The trio was a constant in the world of the Yankees. Robert Merril lived at The Stadium for almost every day game, and for night games when he wasn't singing at the Metropolitan Opera. In his later years he was there for opening day and during the playoffs. Merrill passed on in 2004.

Eddie Layton, whose amazing organ playing kept the game alive, the fans involved, and in many instances kept the Yankees in the game, was also a fixture at The Stadium. During some games, when it appeared that the team needed just that little push, or a Yankee batter needed just that bit of adrenaline to hit that ball where the other team was not, Eddie Layton would manage to get the organ to start to "sing", thus keeping the fans, the Yankees and game exciting and interactive . . . .

Da . . . . da . . . . da . . . . da . . . .
Da . . . . da . . . . da . . . . da . . . .
Da . . . . . da . . . . da . . . . . . da . . . .
Da . . da . . . da . . da
Dadadada . . da . . da . . . .
CHARGE . . . .

Or

Lets go Yankees (clap, clap, clap, clap, clap)
Lets go Yankees (clap, clap, clap, clap, clap)
Lets go Yankees (clap, clap, clap, clap, clap)

Or

Der—ik-jee-ter (clap, clap, clap, clap, clap)

Ber—nee—Will-yams (clap, clap, clap, clap)

Hip—Hip—Horhay (for Posada)

How many times we sang those songs as kids, either at the Stadium or in front of our TV's at home. Our parents grew accustomed to our yelling CHARGE!! from the recesses of our TV rooms, or singing "take me out to the ballgame" along with Eddie Layton on the organ. Interestingly enough, Eddie was originally hired in 1967 to play between innings. During one game early when the Yankee's were losing; having been an old Navy guy, he decided to play the Charge to give the Yankees a "charge". The music worked, Layton got a raise, and the rest is history.

Of great note, Layton had originally turned down the "gig" because he said he knew nothing about baseball, and that the trip from Queens was too difficult since he didn't drive. CBS who owned the Yankees at that time said not to worry they would send a limo for him before each game, and they took their organ star to and from the park for 32 years.

So from the moment Bob Shepard welcomed us to the stadium, to Robert Merrill giving us the goose bumps from his singing the Star Spangled Banner (those goose bumps lasted at least three innings) to Eddie Layton's organ playing who kept us in the game; nowhere in baseball have the fans had a greater team of stadium "entertainment" than those three men who made our Yankee experience so fabled. . . .

The passing of Eddie Layton, and Robert Merrill, and early this season, the absence of Bob Shepherd, no longer permits our stadium experience to be the same. It gives pause to the transition of the team and an era in Yankee history. While Robert Merrill's recording is still played, and we still have stadium entertainment, albeit different, we are no longer held captive by the enormity of talent we have grown accustomed to.

After the tragedies of 9/11 the singing of God Bless America became a mainstay in major league baseball parks, being sung during the 7th inning. Originally written by Irving Berlin while in the Army, it was rejected from the Army camp show, and later picked up by Ms. Smith. Royalties for the song to this day which belong to both Ms. Smith and Mr. Berlin go directly to the Boy Scouts and Girl Scouts of America. Interestingly enough the Yankee have been accused of continuing the tradition since 2001 because they have been quite successful during the inning directly after the singing of God Bless America. I hardly believe that the delay as proposed by the singing of the song gives the Yankees and edge, but perhaps the exhilaration one feels after Kate finishes the song is an emotional boost!!

So we now listen to Kate Smith's recording, and Sinatra or Minelli,'s recoding of NY, NY after the games. We also now have *Cotton Eye Joe*, and *Joey* who lip sinc the Rednex song for us, getting the crowd involved. The dragsters perform their YMCA, and together with all the rest of the sights and sounds none are today as powerful as the combination of Layton and Merrill and Shepard.

YES

Children, who are Yankee fans today, have a decided advantage over our childhood!! They have something special that we never had growing up as Yankee fans, and that is the ability to watch virtually every Yankee game right in their own living rooms. As a child I couldn't wait until the weekends when, if we were lucky, we would be able to see 2 games; often Friday night and Saturday or Sunday afternoon. Sometimes we would get lucky when even some very late nights, when the Yankees were being broadcast from the West Coast starting at 10PM NY time, we could watch our team on TV. Our ability to see the Yankees on TV was severely limited to those games on WPIX 11, or if we were so inclined, to listen on the radio. Having grown up in the television age, and not really accustomed to the radio, Yankee games were a treat to watch.

Today, watching the Yankee games on televisions have is no longer a luxury, but rather a necessity. We rue the days the games are on ESPN or God forbid national television where we are sure Tim McCarver hates our guts and will never broadcast the game fairly. Please give us John Sterling and Suzyn Waldman, and Sweeney Murti who love our Yankees and will give them a fair shake every time.

The YES channel is almost like a gift and the "Yankeeographies", are something special. One Christmas I thnk that I received 7 copies of the latest compilation of Yankeeographies which are excellent pieces each in their own right. The lay claim to the players as people, while revealing parts of their personal life as well as the evolution of their professional baseball lives. None of those videos are more touching that that of Thurman Munson. You almost cry along with Mrs. Munson when you view the plane wreck, or when you acknowledge that Bobby Murcer gave every part of his humanity the day they buried Thurman.

George Steinbrenner and his people recognized the need for the games to be televised, and knew that a whole generation of new fans would come from that advent of the YES network, and I'm sure he is exactly right.

THE COVER

Something special should have been said in the first edition of the book about the cover and the choice of Yankees. During the incredible run that the Yankees had in the late 1990's and early 2000's, there was a nucleus to the team that made it special, that made the team a winner. While much has been said about the players in the body of this book, little has been said about why those players were chosen to grace the cover of the book.

After some consultation with James Fiorentino the fantastic sports artist, and consummate Yankee fan, he and I agreed that the 5 players together with Joe Torre were the "team" that we were talking about, that were the nucleus of those championship years. With Jeter, Posada, Bernie, and Mariano, all Yankees from the start, and the strategic acquisitions of Paul O'Neill and Tino Martinez, the winners were assembled, and thus they grace the cover of this book.

With Paul O'Neill so gracefully slipping into the broadcast booth, and now Tino working for ESPN, it is great to have them around the game, as their insight into baseball and especially into this team is fine!

If you have a desire to have your favorite player gracing your home, go to www.JamesFiorentino.com.

THANK YOU AL

It was another sad moment this Spring when Al Leiter retired from baseball after his return from representing the United States at the World Baseball Classic. Once again in their classy way, the Yankees offered Al a non roster invitation to Spring training, Upon his return to the Yankees Spring Training Camp, Al took the mound one last time threw to one batter who grounded out, and then Al returned the ball to Joe Torre, and said goodbye to the mound, to the field, to the players, and to baseball.

Going out with dignity and grace, Al Leiter had become a huge part of New York fame and fable. Having begun and ended his career as a Yankee, but known mostly for his years playing for the Mets, Al has two World Series rings, one with the Marlins in 1997, and one with Toronto in 1993. He ended his career with 162 wins and 132 losses with an ERA of 3.80 in 419 appearances. After 19 years in the big leagues, Al finally said goodbye to his playing days.

So well known around New York, Al, along with Vinny Testaverde, who was so vocal about the NFL not playing on the Sunday after the 9/11 incident, and many other professional athletes and celebrities helped lead the incredible push after 9/11 to comfort those who had lost loved ones in the terror attacks. Al traveled with many of the players from fire house to fire house, posing for pictures, and putting his arms around those whose sadness could not be contained.

Often referred to as "the mayor", Leiter has often joked about running for elected office. It is likely we will see Al soon, either in the booth analyzing games, on the field analyzing plays as part of a coaching staff, or behind a desk, passing laws that make our lives better.

Goodbye Al!! Thanks for your commitment to baseball, and your commitment to New York! We hope to see you soon!.

GOOD FOR YOU WILLIE!!

It took a very long time for Willie Randolph to get a break as a Manager. With 4 American league Pennants and two World Sries Rings as a player, and 6 American League Pennants and 4 World Series Rings as a coach, Willie has been eminently qualified for a managerial job for some time now. Good for the Mets for giving him the opportunity to coach not only in his home town, but to coach a class team, which will be great contenders for the National League pennant this year.

Willie was passed up by numerous teams before Omar Minaya had great insight to pick Willie. By choosing Willie he has a manager that has won on both sides, as a player and as a coach. He further has someone who has learned from the best in baseball Joe Torre, and he has a New Yorker, and someone who truly understands the players. He knows what the youth of today is all about, and he also knows what tradition can mean to a team.

Willie brings with him great baseball smarts, a level head, and experience under Joe Torre which will prove to be invaluable. A native New Yorker, who knows the town, the media and the players, we wish Willie great success, and hopefully one day soon, he will be back in the Bronx!

THE BIRTH OF A YANKEE FAN

Many people who read the first edition of the book said to me wow, I feel a whole lot more like a Yankee fan than I did before I read the book. That of course is the first clue that a burgeoning Yankee fan is emerging!!

While it is impossible to make someone like something (I learned that a long time ago) it is possible that when one begins to see something the way in which you see it, it can endear them to your way of thinking, to loving what you love. Nowhere was that more evident in my life than in the early 1970's when I watched my 80+ year old Italian grandmother (who barely spoke English) become a Knick fan! Always a baseball fan, I spent most of my high school days playing basketball, which at the time had better playing opportunities for females than softball offered. There was no Title IX and no ability to play Little League or even an organized softball league until I reached high school. Despite my father's insistence and threatened law suits with the Little League officials in Westchester County, I still could not play organized "baseball" with the boys despite my constant playing with them after school and on weekends.

1971 was the year that the Knicks won the championship, and everyone watched those phenomenal players: Walt Frazier, Earl "The Pearl" Monroe, Dave DeBusschere, "Dollar Bill" Bradley, and Willis Read conquer the NBA. While that starting lineup was to die for, and comprised the core of the team; those Knicks who came off the bench were just as engaging, just as important as the starting five. They were: Cazzie Russell with his unorthodox jump shot from the baseline, and Jerry (he who memorized the entire New York City phone book) Lucas, and lastly Phil Jackson, who came off the bench with his flailing arms and legs and good defense to spell the front line.

During that year we watched those Knicks storm through, and by the time the playoffs were at hand, my grandmother would be yelling in Italian at Earl "the Pearl" to "roll" to the basket, or for Willis to get the ball. And while that fabled playoff series where Reed hobbled in the game and gave great inspiration to the team for a tremendous Championship win, there was something that my grandmother identified with, which kept her interest.

She not only developed a fine appreciation for the team, but also for basketball. She learned about the game that season, and watched it often until her death in 1985. She became a FAN.

Fans can be born, and many can become fans later on in life. So many of those around me who have seen my passion for the Yankees were compelled to try to understand what I have been feeling, and thinking with respect to this special affinity. While previously having no experience or desire to watch or participate in anything "sport", I have seen my friends and patients begin to watch the games, to look at the players and to determine that perhaps they need to go to the stadium to look at what I see. Sooner or later many come around to becoming a Yankee fan and loving the game. In fact so many of the children in my practice have become fans, that I can hardly engage in a conversation without the word Yankees coming up.

I believe that there are 5 identifiable ways in which a child becomes a Yankee fan. He/she displays:

1) PASSION
2) IDENTIFICATION
3) REGALIA

PASSION

Passion was something that I defined and identified earlier as a quality which one can not teach, nor acquire. And while passion sets the Yankees aside in many ways as players, one thing I did not state in the original text is that passion is something very special to watch, and it is not confined to the players. While a passionate team is one thing, a passionate fan is another. That passion witnessed can often ignite the "fire in the belly" of another as they actually begin to "see" what you see and "feel" what you feel. Soon that passion is a part of their life.

The transmission of passion in this way is most effective with children, especially in a child who might seemingly not have any interest in baseball. A child can often walk into my office and see the Yankee memorabilia, and then they ask some questions, before long they are looking at the Yankees on television. Then their parents, seeing that they have an interest in the game take then to the Stadium, and soon a Yankee fan is born. I have seen it occur in those children over and over again. A degree of transference takes place, and then they find their very own passion, and their own special reason to be a Yankee fan.

IDENTIFICATION

The need to belong is often strong especially in children. As I have said in the earlier pages of this text is that the team identification with the Yankees is strong and palpable in good seasons and in bad. Children especially love to "dress up" and to wear their opinions on "their sleeves" literally, and thus watching the many young children with Yankee jerseys etc is quite a significant part of their being a Yankee fan.

This identification does not necessarily come from within the family nor does come from being fair-weather fan, as stated earlier, but rather it comes from a genuine "identification" That identification may come from a child who likes a particular player and wants to emulate that player, or from watching the team play, and seeing a player they like, or even meeting a player.

I had a 6 year old come in last year and say to me: "Dr. Joan I'm a 'little bit' a Yankee fan and a 'big bit' a Met fan . . . is that ok"? He went on to say:

"but there is something that we both share, you being a Yankee fan and me being a Met fan". "What is that?" I asked. He said "We both have a Matsui. You have Hideki and I have Kaz". Of course that brought a big smile to my face, as he was right; we both did have a Matsui.

Last week I sat in the diner, and next to me was a group of 10 40+ somethings trying to stump each other on baseball trivia. One asked a question and it was, "Who hit the longest ball in Shea Stadium history?" No one could answer the question. The quizzer gave hints, but still everyone was stumped. My mother, who was sitting next to me said, "Joan, I'm sure you know the answer to that question." I said, "Well, I'm not a baseball trivia nut like so many others, and I certainly am not a Met trivia buff of any kind, but I do know that so many of my peers during the late 1960's wanted to be Tommy Agee, who hit the heck out of the ball and who glided through the outfield in the Met's glory years. I knew about him because of others who identified with him." And the answer was Tommy Agee, and the 10 guys were stunned that I knew the answer, but it was because of childhood identification with the player by my peers that I knew that answer.

REGALIA

We spoke in the text about Birgers and Corfers who wear the regalia of the team when they do well and do not when they do not do well. The Yankee regalia of course is out all season, but especially in the days leading up to the new season when all types of Yankee "garb" can be seen. From the very young child to the older children, to the adults, and "old timers' the Yankee hats, shirts, jackets and other such things like flags and decals on the cars can be seen everywhere in metropolitan New York area.

The Yankee regalia is almost its own subculture, and the new season almost invariably calls for some piece of new clothing to commemorate the beginning of the season. While jerseys, and hats permeate the racks, one now only has to go to the children's section at a major NY department store, or "GO TO MOS" (Modell's) and there is Yankee clothing from the 3-6 month size to adult. The significant amount of Yankee clothing that now comes in the color pink signifies the importance of the female market as baseball fans, something that George Steinbrenner has seriously, as stated earlier, tried to nurture.

The Yankees truly are phenomena. What makes them universally appealing and what allows for them to have fans all over the world is their great appeal as a winner, and as a class organization. The "phenomena" will truly outlive their 27th world championship, and I'm sure in my lifetime I will see the 30th, or maybe more . . . .

The thing about baseball is that nothing is assured, and nothing can be taken for granted. That being said . . . .

Go Yankees!

Bring Home

27

JAMES FIORENTINO

At the age of fifteen, James was the youngest artist ever to be featured in the National Baseball Hall of Fame and Museum for his likeness of Reggie Jackson, which was hung beside the paintings of Norman Rockwell and Andy Warhol. His painting commemorating Roberto Clemente is currently featured and will remain as part of their permanent collection.

As the youngest artist inducted into the prestigious New York Society of Illustrators in 1998, along with Rockwell, Pyle, Wyeth, Kent Peaks, Holland, and Fuchs, James continues to prove his achievements as a highly regarded illustrator and painter.

James has also been featured on such national and regional television shows as: ABC World New, CBS This Morning, ESPN's Baseball Magazine, Fox After Breakfast, and Madison Square Garden Network's New York Yankee Magazine Show.

James has painted portraits for most of the Yankees past and present including Joe Torre, Derek Jeter, Don Mattingly, Don Zimmer, Jason Giambi, Robinson Cano, and Alex Rodriguez. Further he has painted portraits of stars and luminaries such as Mother Teresa, Mikael Gorbachev, and Michael Jordan.

www.JamesFiroentino.com

DR. JOAN FALLON

Dr. Joan Fallon, a former assistant professor at Yeshiva University and presently CEO of CureMark, a biotechnology company, is a life-long Yankee fan and student of the game. With two major passions in her life baseball and children; "Dr. Joan" as she is called, has passed on her love of baseball and the Yankees to two generations of children in her chiropractic pediatric office. A nationally-ranked squash player in college, "one-on-one" champion in High School and the first female to enter the Westchester County Junior golf tournament, sports has always been a big part of her life. She has been honored to have a letter written to Mickey Mantle chosen for his farewell book: *Letters To Mickey*, as well as having authored numerous professional texts and papers. She takes great pride in her chiropractic pediatric practice as she is able to help numerous children, many of whom have developmental disabilities. As a patent holder and CEO of CureMark she hopes to bring significant help to children with ADD, ADHD, and autism in the very near future. She is currently part of the committee which is helping to put together the handicapped amenities for the "New Yankee Stadium".

REFERENCES

Anderson, Dave, ed. 2002. *The New York Yankees illustrated history*. New York: St. Martin's Press.

Eig, Jonathan. 2005. *Luckiest man: The life and death of Lou Gehrig*. New York: Simon & Schuster.

Funk, D, and J. James. The psychological continuum model: A conceptual framework for understanding an individual's psychological connection to sport. *Sport Management Review*, 4(2), 119-150.

———. The fan attitude network (FAN) model: Exploring attitude formation and change among sport consumers. *Sport Management Review*, 7 (1), 1-26.

Gentile, Derek. 2004. *The complete New York Yankees: The total encyclopedia of the team*. New York: Black Dog & Leventhal.

Hayes, RK; 2003. God Bless America, Land That I Love. *http://katesmith.org/gba.html* (accessed June 1, 2006)

Hills, Matt. 2002. *Fan cultures (Sussex studies in culture and communication)*. New York: Routledge.

http://en.wikipedia.org/wiki/Bob_Shepherd Biography of Bob Shepherd (accessed May 17, 2006)

http://en.wikipedia.org/wiki/Omar_Minaya Biography of Omar Minaya (accessed May 17, 2006)

http://www.msnbc.msn.com/id/6332624/ AP Press Release. Robert Merrill (accessed June 1, 2006)

http://www.sing365.com/music/lyric.nsf/Rednex-Biography. Biography of Rednex (accessed May 17, 2006) *http://www.spaceagepop.com/layton.htm. 2006.* Eddie Layton Biography. (accessed May 17, 2006)

Jeter, Derek. 2005. Turn 2 Foundation. http://derekjeter.mlb.com/NASApp/mlb/players/jeter_derek/turn2/index.jsp (accessed January 12, 2005).

Locke, Brad. 2004. Heart of sports: Fan psychology 101. http://headlines.agapepress.org/archive/6/12004bl.asp (accessed February 2, 2005).

Madrigal, R., and J. James. Team quality and the home advantage. *Journal of Sports Behavior*, 22 (3), 381-398.

Mantle, M., and friends and family of Mickey Mantle. 1995. *Letters to Mickey by the friends and family of Mickey Mantle.* New York: Harper Collins.

Mantle, M., and H. Gluck. *The Mick.* 1986. 2nd ed. New York: Jove.

Mueller, D. 2005. Intergroup relations research. http://www.users.muohio.edu/muelledg/social_identity_theory_research.htm

Olshan, J. 2004. Inside Queens: Yankee organist. Queens Tribune Archives. *http://www.queenstribune.com* (accessed June 1, 2006)

Queenan, Joseph. 2003. *True believers: The tragic inner life of sports.* New York: Holt.

Torre, Joe. 2005. My story. Safe at Home Foundation. http://www.joetorre.org/kids_story.html (accessed July 7, 2005).

——. 2005. Safe at Home Foundation. http://www.joetorre.org (accessed July 7, 2005).

Trail, G., and J. James. The motivation scale for sport consumption: The comparison of psychometric properties with other sport motivation scales. *Journal of Sports Behavior*, 24 (1), 108-127.

Vancil, Mark, and Mark Mandrake, eds. 2003. *The New York Yankees: One hundred years, the official retrospective.* New York: Ballantine.

Wann, Daniel, ed. 2001. *Sport fans: The psychology and social impact of spectators.* New York: Routledge.

Wann, D., et. al. 1993. Sports fans: Measuring degree of identification with their team. *International Journal of Sports Psychology*, 24 (1), 5-6.

Wann, D., et al. Assessing the psychological well-being of sports fans using the profiles of mood states: The importance of team identification. International Sports Journal, 3 (1), 84-85.

www.nba.com.2006. National Basketball Association Biography of Dave DeBusschere. *http://aol.nba.com/history/players/debusschere_summary.html* (accessed May 17, 2006)

www.yankees.com. 2005. New York Yankees. http://newyork.yankees.mlb.com/NASApp/mlb/index.jsp?c_id=nyy (accessed January 1, 2005).